GOD FOR AN OLD MAN

GOD FOR AN OLD MAN

Thomas M. Dicken

RESOURCE *Publications* · Eugene, Oregon

GOD FOR AN OLD MAN

Resource Publications
An Imprint of Wipf and Stock Publishers
199 W. 8th Ave., Suite 3
Eugene, OR 97401

www.wipfandstock.com

ISBN 13: 978-1-4982-3894-6

Manufactured in the U.S.A.   12/15/2015

For my two Anchors in life

My wife Nancy

and

My son John

CONTENTS

ACKNOWLEDGEMENTS

Over the years, I have been able to work through my thoughts about some important topics in academic journals. I am grateful to all those journals for enabling my work to go ahead. Inevitably, the result of those years is implicit in this book.

In some places, that earlier work is very explicit in these pages. My concluding chapter originally appeared in 2015 as "God for an Old Man" in *Process Studies*. My chapter "Dying: An Interim Report" first appeared in *Soundings: An Interdisciplinary Journal*. I had been told in May, 2006 that I had lymphoma, and perhaps had a year to live. I needed to write about that. I wrote my essay in August, 2006. I'm glad I did and I'm glad my article appeared in *Soundings* and is also in this book.

I have been working through my ideas for over fifty years. My article "The Homeless God" in the *Journal of Religion* was a breakthrough for me, allowing me to break with the last constraints of a traditional view of God as omnipresent and strike out on my own, finding my own way. The four chapters in the "Adult Thoughts" portion of the book have developed from ideas first explored in that article. My chapter on John Updike's *Seek My Face* develops insights first explored in part of my article "God and Pigment: John Updike on the Conservation of Meaning" in *Religion and Literature* in 2004.

Paragraphs and pages from other articles also appear, scattered throughout these pages, though none of those is reprinted here in such detail. The articles were influential and suggestive as I wrote this book. In particular my thoughts about art and literature emerged in various articles. All of my relevant journal articles are listed in the Bibliography section of this book.

All biblical quotations are from the *New Revised Standard Version.*

INTRODUCTION

When I was one year old, in 1937, the Ohio River flooded major sections of Louisville. Disease seemed to spread in the many disruptions caused by that flood. I contracted diphtheria. Inoculations for diphtheria were available back then, but my family tended to avoid medical care, influenced both by poverty and a belief that God would take care of us.

Several times during my childhood, my mother would tell me how close I had come to dying. Dr. Craddock, the physician who had delivered me at childbirth in our home a year earlier, was finally called. He came to our house and told my mother that my life was in the balance. It could go either way.

When my mother told me this story, she said that she had gone out for a walk around the block, praying as she went. She told God she could not stand it any more. God should either let me die or heal me. When she returned to our small house, Dr. Craddock told her my fever had broken. He thought that I would survive. My mother explained to me that God had spared me in response to her prayer. That meant that God had a purpose for me.

That was an impressive story to be told as a child. I listened to my mother carefully, but kept my own questions to myself. Why had I had to go through all that if my life was part of God's purpose? How did prayer work? What did the story tell me about my mother? About God? I filed the story away, but that account provoked my first thoughts about God.

I have thought about God throughout my life, reading philosophical and theological works about God, but also reading novels and memoirs that had suggestions about God. I have been involved with churches, both Pentecostal and liberal Protestant churches. I have also had long periods of not being involved with any church. I never lost interest in God, however. I have published a number of articles in academic journals, developing my thoughts and opening myself to the responses of others.

In recent years, I have become preoccupied with my own life story and how thoughts about God have interacted with events in my life. I have never before written in any responsible way about my life and my ongoing interaction with the thought of God. I attempt to do that here.

Since I think that human life does, in fact, have various definable stages, I have tried to understand how my ideas of God were influenced at several stages of life. The God I find interesting in my eighth decade of exploring, thinking, and experiencing is different from the God I found interesting in my tenth year. I have pondered the ideas of the great Erik Erikson, who saw human life as being defined by eight stages. He saw old age as a time for wisdom, learned over the years, teaching children by example that life is well worth living. In this brief book, I have four major sections: Young Impressions, Adult Thoughts, Side Views (art and literature), and God for an Old Man, in which I discuss what God means and does not mean for me as I wind down that eighth decade. If my "Young Impressions" might be described as looking in a rear view mirror, my collection "Side Views" reflects my glances in side view mirrors, describing two of the major influences on my life: art and literature.

I have been influenced over the years by process thought, a vision of reality articulated originally by Alfred North Whitehead and Charles Hartshorne in the twentieth century and developed in detail by many philosophers, theologians, and other thinkers since then. In my own academic writing, I have made a small contribution to this effort.

I have made my own critiques of some aspects of this school of thought. Both the influence of this vision on my views and my occasional differences with this vision will surface in this book. They are also spelled out in more precise language in academic articles I have published over the years, particularly articles in the journal *Process Studies*.

I also want to say something about existentialism, the school of thought that influenced philosophical and theological thought, as well as art, literature, and memoir, in the post-World War II era. I was deeply influenced by many of those thinkers. Other schools of thought have become dominant over the years, but I continue to judge ideas from many thoughtful writers in terms of their existential impact. Today, we are perhaps more inclined to talk about the "personal" meaning or impact of an idea, rather than the "existential" meaning. This book contains much reflection about God. Some people talk about a "personal God." As our thoughts about God become more abstract, reaching out to eons of time, abstract cosmic purposes, and extraordinary distances, the personal God begins to fade. I don't believe we can talk about a personal God without talking about ourselves in a personal way. Those of us in the academic world tend to be shy about being too personal. In this book, I have written in a more personal way than I ever have. I have been influenced by process thought and existential thought. Most importantly, I have been shaped in my thought by my own life.

PART I

YOUNG IMPRESSIONS

1 DISRUPTION

We lived in a shotgun house, with rooms leading directly to one another, with no hallways: living room, bedroom, kitchen, bath. An ell had been built in back, adding a second bedroom. My favorite place was a roofed but unscreened porch behind the house, which one walked down to by two steps from the kitchen. The space served as my mother's laundry, with an old-fashioned second-hand washer out there. Two rollers on top of the washer allowed a person to squeeze water out of the washed clothes, which were then hung up on a clothesline to dry. A rod stuck out the side of the washer that started the agitator, which swirled the clothes in the washer. The washer was an avocado green, showing its age in chipped paint. The agitator rod was missing the knob that would have provided a handle, leaving only the iron rod itself. There was a flat door on the porch that opened to stairs, leading to the coal cellar. Coal was delivered at the beginning of winter and my father would bring up several lumps at a time, placing the bucket next to the stove in the main bedroom that provided heat for the house. My parents did not like for me to go down into the cellar, since it was dirty with coal dust. For me, the pit of darkness was mysterious as I stood watching my father go down with his flashlight to get a bucket of coal.

Beyond those practical uses, the porch space was my fantasy lab. I often played by myself, imagining myself as the main figure in any number of dramas. The washing machine could be "the car over there" in which my imagined cohorts and I would make our getaway. Having a dungeon to which I might consign uncooperative spies also helped. As I watch my grandchildren with their busy lives full of highly programmed (and expensive) events, I wonder about their possible loss of fantasy time alone with themselves. I loved my porch.

If a person grows up in Louisville, Kentucky, Derby Day is part of the church calendar. Typically, that involves a sermon the Sunday before the first Saturday in May warning of the many ways one might be tempted to sin during the upcoming weekend. On Derby Day in 1944, my parents and I sat around the small table in the kitchen, talking about the race that would take place in the afternoon. It was a beautiful Saturday. Since my father usually worked at two jobs, I enjoyed having both my parents present, talking about the chances of various horses.

My parents began to get busy with their tasks and I bounced out the back door, down the first step, and then leaped, as I often did, over onto the flat cellar door, planning to bounce off it onto the flat surface of the porch. However, I did this at the exact moment the meter reader was lifting the door to go down to the cellar, to read our electric meter. I was thrown through the air by my own momentum, my direction diverted by the lifted cellar door, into the naked rod of the washing machine, which penetrated my cheek.

The laws of physics held true. A happy eight-year-old boy bouncing happily on the first step down, leaping over onto the more-or-less horizontal door of the cellar, a maneuver he had done many times before, at the exact instant that a meter reader was lifting the door, throwing the boy against the washing machine, where the exposed metal rod went into his left cheek. Yet, what I took from that moment was not a respect for physics, but rather an awareness that the accidental is always there, the conjoining of many separate and seemingly unrelated lines of force. No matter how causally determined things might be by brute laws of physics, the coming together of so many obvious, trivial events was itself a matter of chance. Always, anything, anything at all, can happen.

Some of these contingencies in my life have been wonderful and I have wondered whether the odd coming together of things in a wonderful way might be called grace. Other such events cry out for some other less joyful term. Another contingency that day was that the horse that won the Kentucky Derby later that day was named Pensive.

Since then, as an adult, I have thought of the meter reader, whose day started off happily enough, a perfect May day to make his rounds and suddenly there was a child there with a hole in his face.

That event had an impact on my own very personal sense of *causality* in life, but also of my own *substance*: I could be penetrated. The very thin boy with a scar on his cheek: that was my substance.

Other basic categories, such as *time* and *space*, also take on profoundly personal meanings. Philosophers speak of the categories of substance, causality, time and space. For each of us, those categories are not mere abstractions. They give form to our sense of things as we move through life. That is, if we are pensive enough.

It is a world of tragic contingency, yet meetings that seem to be filled with grace also occur. There is an incomprehensible brutality of existence and an astonishing tenderness. All these aspects are ways we experience fundamental categories of time, space, substance, and causality. Some losses are never recovered; some gifts are lasting.

Once I had time to reflect on what had happened to me, I realized that no one was to blame. So many things had to come together all at once, a moment in time and dimensions of space that would be impossible to reproduce. A few years later I began to think of this event as a "contingency." Everything about it could have been different. Throughout life, there are many contingencies. Everything could be different. Many contingencies are wonderful events. When they are wonderful contingencies, we sometimes call them "grace." I have read scientists who claim that if we started the universe all over again from another Big Bang, there are so many contingencies that a different universe would emerge, standing in contrast to any random moment in the path of our present universe.

I read writers carefully to see how they assume or talk about the nature of contingency, about time and space, substance and causality.

2 TRAUMA AND GRACE

EMBODIED INSIGHT

Some insights slowly emerge and change things over a significant period of time. Humans go through periods of trauma, when their very being is damaged. Healing from trauma is slow and painful, whether it is caused by physical trauma, verbal abuse, abandonment, confinement, terror, or deep loss. Dictionary definitions tend to stress trauma caused by a physical wound. However, in recent years, we have become more aware of the trauma associated with war. Even when the soldier survives without an obvious physical wound, we have begun to use the term "trauma" more inclusively.

The four major categories into which our human experience of life can be analyzed (time, space, substance, and causality) become crucial for understanding and assessing a person's basic sense of life.

In her book *Trauma and Grace*, Serene Jones does not mention these categories as a distinct topic. This makes her work with traumatized people (mostly women) that much more convincing. The categories are used in the most natural way as the best possible description of what is going on. Trauma is a name for deep disruptions in our sense of our own *substance*, our *causal* role in events, our sense of surrounding *space*, and our apprehension or sense of lived *time*.

A powerful example is found in Jones' work with women who are unable to bring a child to term, much as they might try.

"Women have told me that along with their inability to make a child comes a sense of their inability to make a future": a very personal and existential sense of time. For these women, Jones writes, "time stretches before them as a story of parching barrenness or violent bloodiness."

This death of hope and expectancy has a spatial counterpart, a "rupturing of self." There is often dissolution of bodily borders. Jones writes, "By 'borders,' I refer to those morphological lines that mark the difference between the outside and the inside of self. In the throes of reproductive loss, women often describe a feeling of not knowing where they physically end and where the outside world begins. This is because their insides are quite literally falling out."[1]

Obviously, these meanings shade into a given woman's loss of a sense of her own substance and her ability to be a causal agent. She becomes fragmented and dispersed, as if she had been leaking into the world. Her fragmentation means she leaves pieces of herself "in rags, in toilets, in medical waste cans."[2]

Jones describes other traumatized women, victims of rape, abuse, or loss. Running through her scenarios is the language of time, space, substance, and causality (or the rupture of all these), without lapsing into technical, philosophical language. She stays close to the hurt and loss described by these traumatized victims.

Jones' most careful statement of this structure summarizes one woman in this way: "(1) Instead of experiencing herself as an agent, the woman grieving reproductive loss knows herself as powerless to stop it and yet guilty for her perceived failure. (2) As her hope dies, she also becomes a self without a future. (3) She is a self, whose borders are as fluid as the blood she cannot stanch, a self undone. (4) And in the space of this undoing, she is the anti-material self who does not give life; she takes it away."[3]

Daunting as some philosophical categories might be, Jones uses them to yield insight into the real nature of lived experience.

1. Jones, *Trauma and Grace*, 137.
2. Ibid., 138.
3. Ibid., 139.

The disruption of trauma is a rupturing or shattering of these categories.

Grace in these traumatic circumstances moves slowly, healing very gradually. Healing often happens, if it happens, in a group of other traumatized people, listened to and guided by a sensitive leader. Perhaps none of us is ever healed completely. I believe, however, that having a sense of God's presence is not a merely spiritual or ethereal experience. It is something that offers us a different take on or a different way of seeing our very being, in all its substantial, causal, temporal and spatial structures. Though we do not need to use technical language, we need to be aware of the intrinsic change in how we experience ourselves in the presence of God.

Stories such as those told by Jones suggest that we need to be very careful in our language about God. The penumbra around the word "presence" needs to be monitored carefully in our language. Though language about God often thoughtlessly presupposes a male God, Jones points out that, at such times, lifting up prayer to " 'Mother God' seemed a cruel joke."[4] We need to do caring, careful searches for the best ways to express our deepest experiences.

To explore trauma as a realm that may be entered by grace, we need to be aware of the very physical or embodied aspects of both trauma and grace. Trauma clinicians, Jones reminds us, speak of "the visceral traces left behind by traumatic events, traces like quick-startle responses, headaches, exhaustion, muscle aches, distractibility, and depression—all of which sporadically haunted my own interior world. If the aftermath of violence was this visceral, I reasoned, it made sense that grace capable of touching it should be equally physical."[5]

Most religions do suggest muscular, embodied ways of being in the presence of God: kneeling, prostrating oneself, standing, bowing, singing, raising one's arms. To be in God's presence is not merely a "high-end" experience. There are even stories about how, in the presence of God, we may be ordered to take off the shoes

4. Ibid., 127.
5. Ibid., 158.

from our feet (Exodus 3:5). Insight into God is an embodied, visceral experience, not merely an intellectual hunch.

3 THE SUMMER OF '45

I still remember the summer of 1945. I was in love with Anna Laurie, and her husband, Joe, was my best friend. I think all three of us had a pretty good idea of how I felt, but no one seemed to have a problem with it.

There are snapshots from those summer days that are sharp and clear in my mind, just as there are many details that I probably didn't bother to get straight in the first place. And there are emotions I can still evoke simply by remembering.

Most summers, I would visit my grandparents for a few days on their farm just outside Glasgow, Kentucky. Sometimes it might be a week or so. This particular summer must have been one of my longer visits, maybe two or three weeks, but I wasn't noticing such details. As far as I was concerned, a world war might be drawing to a close without impinging on my nine-year-old life.

Joe and Anna Laurie lived in a shack on my grandfather's farm with their three or four children. I never got all the children straight, since they were all too young for me to play with. Joe worked for my grandfather, though their arrangement was also one of those things that didn't interest me. Looking back, I imagine that both Joe and Anna Laurie must have been in their mid-twenties. I never thought to ask them how old they were, though their first question to me each summer was to ask how old I had gotten to be, then beaming as if my age was the most extraordinary thing either of them had ever heard.

Sometimes I would go along with my grandfather to do "chores," which was the name for all the work that went on around the farm. When I returned each summer to Louisville, my mother would not let me refer to anything I did around the house as a chore, telling me it wasn't that hard to do, so I have always associated the word with farm work. I preferred doing chores with Joe, however, who was more fun than my grandfather. He treated me as an equal, telling me what "we" were going to have to do next and sometimes asking my opinion about things. I was always thrilled when I got the answer right. Joe would say "That's right," as if that was as extraordinary a fact as my age.

Most of Anna Laurie's work kept her confined to the house with the children, though she let me come and visit and talk with her. I marveled that so many people lived in the small house, though I never thought about why that might be. When Joe came home to take a nap or do work around the house, she would go out on the farm to do chores. I joined her whenever we went to pick damson plums from the orchard. We would take several buckets with us and my grandfather would pay us a quarter for each bucket we filled. Anna Laurie made me be careful as I climbed up into a plum tree, holding my bucket for me till I got up. She climbed up after me and found a secure branch opposite me to nestle into. We would start picking, with Anna Laurie picking four or five times faster than I did. I would look around for a plum, then pick it. Anna Laurie would have one hand moving towards a cluster of plums while the other hand was emptying three or four plums into the bucket. Occasionally, she would drop three of four plums in my bucket and give me a big smile.

Her smile is one of my mental snapshots. She had a wide mouth and her teeth glistened white. She had very pronounced cheekbones which seemed to stand out even more when she smiled. To this day, I notice the cheekbones of women. She wore a bright bandanna around her black hair. I suppose that today I would describe her eyes as sultry, though that certainly was not a word that came to my mind in 1945. I simply noticed that her eyes were different from any I had ever seen. She wore ragged jeans and a flowered blouse. Back then, even my grandmother made "sun dresses," as she called them, out of the feed bags, which had bright designs for that very purpose.

Picking damson plums with Anna Laurie was something I had done for several years, but this was the summer I fell in love with her. I noticed myself noticing her in a different way. When she leaned over me to reach a cluster of plums, I inhaled deeply, loving the human smells of skin and sweat and something else, something not perfume but better than that, something clean and deserving of a deep breath.

This was the summer that it hit me in a decisive way that women were more beautiful than men. It was a couple more years before I noticed that girls were more beautiful than boys, but I knew that Anna Laurie was something unlike and better than anything that was male. Anna Laurie had a way of reaching forward for a bunch of plums and her blouse would loosen at the top and there would be the very top beginning of a swelling of her breasts. Her skin was the color of the chocolate milk I still preferred to white milk. It was not so much sexual desire that I experienced, but more of a dizziness, an enchantment with that very moment. To this day, if I notice damson plum jam on a grocery shelf, I can experience the identical dizziness, a desire to lose myself in the moment. Sometimes Anna Laurie would notice me looking. She would reach up and adjust the top of her blouse, all the while giving me the biggest, most wonderful smile.

One day we returned to their house and Joe asked me if I wanted to go to the movies with him on Saturday night. I knew that Joe often went into town on Saturday nights, while Anna Laurie stayed home with the children. She may have had her own night to go into town while Joe stayed with the children, but that was one of the details I didn't bother to get straight. There was a Tom Mix cowboy movie scheduled to be shown at the Trigg Theater. Of course, there would also be a B grade movie in addition to the feature, newsreels, cartoons, previews of "coming attractions," and perhaps a "short subject," as they were called. I was really excited the whole next day. It seemed very grown-up to be going to a movie with a friend, instead of with parents.

Joe drove an old car purchased by my grandfather (who either didn't or couldn't drive), so that Joe could drive my grandfather around and run errands for him. We drove the five miles up the Burkesville Pike into Glasgow. Joe bought the two tickets at the window outside the theater, then he bought me some popcorn. Then he said something to me that still stings each time I remember it.

"Tommy, you go on in and find you a seat. After the movies are over, you come right back to this spot, right here, and I'll be here."

I blinked up at him. "Aren't you going to come with me?"

Joe shook his head. "I'm going up into the balcony to find a seat with the other coloreds."

"Can't you sit down here with me?" I asked.

"No," he said. "That's just the way they do things. You go along now. Do you need to go to the bathroom first? I'll be right here when you come out."

He gave me a little shove and I walked into the big, dark theater. I don't remember anything about the Tom Mix movie that night, though I could describe the plots of dozens of other Tom Mix movies. I sat there trying to figure some other things out.

Later that night, Joe was indeed waiting for me. He asked if I had had a good time and I nodded. I didn't say a word driving home with him. There are many questions I wish I had asked him, but that night I simply sat there thinking. I had discovered that summer that the world is a strange place, filled with both some wonderful mysteries I was just beginning to explore and with some craziness I was determined to change.

4 ABYSS

THE ULTIMACY OF INSIGHT

I had been begging my father to let me look down the well at my grandmother's farm, which we visited a couple of times a year. In the 1940s, only the first floor of the old farmhouse had electricity. We had kerosene lamps to read by in the bedrooms on the second floor. Chamber pots and an outhouse were more of a curiosity to me than an inconvenience. And water from the well was brought into the house in big buckets. We all used a shared ladle to help ourselves to a drink. It was coldest and tastiest when a fresh bucket had just been hauled up.

The well itself was a few yards from the back porch. The concrete platform was raised a foot or so off the ground and a top made from wooden planks covered the hole. A bucket would be attached to a rope and gradually lowered into the water by turning the wooden handle of the round bar that was over the hole. I watched the grownups turn the handle to lower the bucket, then turn it to raise the filled bucket. I wanted to see what it was like down there.

I don't remember how many times I had begged to be able to look down the well. Finally, my father gripped my legs and let me rest my body on the platform. I couldn't see anything; it was just dark. Dad let me move a few inches closer to the hole. He told me to look straight down. I still couldn't see anything. One more inch and the instruction to straighten out my body and to look *straight* down. And there it was: it was round and shiny. Dad told me it was the sky reflecting up from the water. It was bright and beautiful. I couldn't believe anything could be that far down. It was the first time I ever experienced awe.

I was informed that if I ever moved the top and did that on my own, I would get a spanking I would never forget. It took a few days before I found a good time to go back and do all that on my own.

In a very different mood, Helen Vendler discusses the attempts by the poet Emily Dickinson to define the indefinable, such as dreadful, unremitting pain. This kind of pain consumes a person's very substance and can only be described as an abyss of pain.[1]

I have never endured this kind of abyssal pain, having experienced only sharp, sudden pains that were relieved within a bearable amount of time by medical intervention. However, I have spent hours over the years visiting people in pain treatment centers of hospitals and other specialized facilities. In the rooms sealed off from sound and light, I said trivial things, offered clumsy prayer, listened carefully to almost inaudible responses, and always asked if the person in the abyss wanted me to return or to leave them free of having to deal with me. Always, from the abyss, they said they wanted me to return. Even though my presence must have added to their disturbance and pain, they chose the presence over the abyss.

Today, the word "abyss" more often points to an existential emptiness, the oblivion of death or the vacuum of meaning. It is possible for us to see ourselves as surrounded by emptiness, rather than as surrounded by the presence of God.

Jorge Luis Borges writes that Blaise Pascal was perhaps the first modern human to sense the ultimate implications of the early revolutionary discoveries in astronomy. If astronomers such as Giordano Bruno were liberated by these discoveries, Pascal found the "deep space" and "deep time" that were being revealed to be frightening. The awesome space "became a labyrinth and an abyss for Pascal. He abhorred the universe and would have liked to adore

---

1. Vendler, *Dickinson*, 231–233.

God; but God, for him, was less real than the abhorred universe."[2] The human sense of an abyss or a "deep" may have originated with the sea, and continued into the implicit world-perspective of Herman Melville's novel *Moby Dick*, but Pascal already knew that same fearful, fascinating dizziness could now also be experienced by simply looking at the sky. Perhaps for the first time, a human found himself torn between looking at the abyss in the sky and seeking after God.

Christian Wiman writes of the tension involved in exploring his recently rediscovered faith in God, while also trying to explain to himself and to others that all the doubt, all the uncertainty, and all the anxiety about his cancer, remains.[3] He writes of a beginning of a poem on which he has worked: "My God my bright abyss / Into which all my longing will not go / Once more I come to the edge of all I know / And believing nothing believe in this:"

But the poem does not move beyond this point. He can't force it to move. Of course, the reader notices the paradox of a "bright abyss." It is perhaps like a tiny wet circle of reflected sky. The only way to speak of God, for some of us at least, is to speak paradoxically of the abyss. It may be that we are more certain of the abyss than we are of God. A "bright abyss" captures something of what we need to say. Such faith is not like anything that typically gets flaunted as faith. But Wiman can conclude, as he reflects on his fragment of a poem, that "I seem to see you in the black flower mourners make beside a grave I do not know, in the ember's innards like a shining hive, in the bare abundance of a winter tree whose every limb is lit and fraught with snow."[4] Wiman has described the oddity of what it is like to find God in the abyss. He suggests three images. "The bare abundance of a winter tree" comes closest to describing how I might understand what an abyssal God is like. There is one more line: "Lord, Lord, how bright the abyss inside that 'seem.'" I search back for the "seem" and find it in the "I seem to see you. . . ." The word "seem" has the slippage, the

2. Borges, *Non-Fictions*, 353.

3. Wiman, *My Bright Abyss*, 3.

4. Ibid., 13.

fracturing, and the slant we need if we are going to speak of God. Only a word like "seem" will let us back into God from the abyss.

5 HOMELESSNESS

I have never actually been homeless. My closest approach to that condition was in 1946. During the war years, the federal Office of Price Administration (OPA) had stabilized prices, both income and costs. My family could afford the $20 a month rent for the shotgun house on Garland Avenue in Louisville. My parents used the living room as a bedroom, my older sister used the bedroom, we ate in the kitchen, and my bedroom was the ell room. For the two years of 1943–44, however, an Italian family, who were working in one of the many war-related factories in Louisville, took over my bedroom for themselves and their daughter, who was about my age. I moved in with my sister. We sometimes took turns eating in the small kitchen and other times we all ate together in the kitchen.

When the war ended in 1945, however, the OPA began to step aside and the market began to take over. Many young men and some young women returned from their military life, eager to get married and start a family, as well as taking advantage of the GI Bill to start college. There was a boom as housing developments sprang up everywhere to accommodate this return and the process of "beginning life." Jobs turned from the war effort to the new possibilities of a long-restrained society. This was back in the day when nations and people had actually noticed that a war was going on. The mood of the nation was upbeat, glad to see its young people return, glad to see an economic boom.

However, all this played out differently for my family. My father was not a young veteran. Our landlord raised the rent substantially on our house, tripling the cost. We had to find something cheaper. It turned out to be two rooms on the third floor of a once-attractive private home on Third Street, which had been subdivided into rental rooms. The bathroom, shared with another family, was on the second floor. The house was not air-conditioned, so we ran a small fan to circulate the air in the summer. My parents used one room, my sister and I the other room.

My mother soon began to walk around the neighborhood, knocking on doors as she tried to find something better for us that we could afford. Several times she found something, but the resident owner looked at the gangly ten-year-old with her and told her they did not accept children. "He is very quiet and well behaved," my mother would say, as I stood there trying to look very quiet and well behaved.

Though I have never been homeless, I learned in those years that even when things are going well for many people, those who have the least resources are often not able to share in the opportunities available to many other people.

Eventually the boom that improved the lives of many Americans also improved the conditions of our family. My father made a little more money and my parents moved us into a house where I had my own private space, in the attic in the winter and in the basement in the summer.

I was never homeless, but I did learn to treasure my ability, as I became self-supporting, to have a quiet, private space to myself. My personal sense of what space is like was affected by those childhood spaces. Looking back, it is probably not surprising that I chose to live in spacious Montana for 22 years as an adult.

PART II

ADULT THOUGHTS

6 THE HOMELESS GOD

Some thinkers have defined God as almighty (omnipotent), all-knowing (omniscient), and in all places (omnipresent). However, there are many problems and conundrums with such views. In most theological thought, *omnipresence* tends to receive less attention than omnipotence and omniscience. It hangs out with them as their weak sibling. This may be because the other two themes clearly figure in major theological debates. Omnipotence is often discussed in the context of *theodicy*, attempts to solve the problem of evil. If God is both good and all-powerful, why does evil exist? Thinkers produce many variations on what might be meant by omnipotence, in order to resolve this problem. Omniscience also often figures in discussions of theodicy. If God knows everything, surely a better world could be designed. But omniscience also plays into discussions of the nature of time and eternity. If God knows the future in detail, is there any human freedom to choose or change the future? What happens to human responsibility? If the future is already known, is it really *future*? Is it all really one big eternal Now, in which past, present, and future are dissolved into God's present? Again, much attention has been devoted to these issues, though I am not preoccupied with such issues.

Other thinkers have suggested that God acts in the world by "luring," rather than by causing everything. God knows everything there is to know (at any given moment), but God's knowledge *grows as there is more to be known.* This approach is based on the idea of spontaneity and freedom in the world, a world that is therefore open to being shaped. This view has been worked out in detail by philosophers and theologians influenced by Alfred North Whitehead and Charles Hartshorne, known as "process thinkers."

This view of God as deeply *open to* and *influenced by* the universe is referred to by these process thinkers as the "contingent" nature of God, since God's being and becoming are shaped by the contingent universe. God *as such*, without any reference to or influence by the world, is often called the "primordial" nature of God, God as defined only by Godself. On the other hand, God as influenced by the many contingencies of the world is known as the "contingent" nature of God. I am myself much more interested in this contingent description of God, rather than in speculating about God's primordial nature. I have been interested in contingencies ever since I fell onto the washing machine as a child.

I am also deeply interested in a set of ideas that began to come together for me when I first read Dietrich Bonhoeffer's *Letters and Papers from Prison*. Dietrich Bonhoeffer, a brilliant theologian, spent months in prison at the end of World War II, after he had been arrested by the Nazi government for taking part in attempts to weaken Hitler's evil rule, finally planning with others an attempt to assassinate Hitler. During that time in prison, he wrote many remarkable letters to his friend Eberhard Bethge, hinting at a dazzling array of ideas. He did not live to develop them in detail, since he was executed days before the end of the war. Bonhoeffer hints at ideas about "religionless Christianity," the need to take responsibility in "a world come of age," Jesus as "the man for others," and the dangers of explaining God in terms of what we don't know, rather than in terms of what we do know, a tendency which he described as a "God of the gaps." These provocative few pages have haunted and influenced Christian thought for several generations. We never know for sure, of course, as we develop one or another of these ideas, whether our development has very much to do with what Bonhoeffer might have done with the same phrases, if he had lived. In some ways, the power of these phrases derives from their epigrammatic nature. Yet these phrases have been fertile, shifting the thoughts of many of us away from established lines of thought into new paths.

Among Bonhoeffer's most provocative suggestions were thoughts about God's powerlessness. Bonhoeffer wrote, "God allows himself to be edged out of the world and on to the cross. God is weak and powerless in the world, and that is exactly the way, the only way, in which he can be with us and help us. . .. (I)t is not by his omnipotence that Christ helps us, but by his weakness and suffering." Often, he writes, a person wants a *deus ex machina*, a powerful, problem-solving God. "The Bible however directs him to the powerlessness and suffering of God; only a suffering God can help." Otherwise, Bonhoeffer wrote, we end up with a God of the gaps, a God who prevents humans from coming of age, from taking full responsibility for their lives.[1]

The fundamental biblical text for this approach might be Paul's claim that "God chose what is foolish in the world to shame the wise, God chose what is weak in the world to shame the strong" (1 Corinthians 1:27).

"The foolishness of God" is a critique (perhaps influenced by Paul's time in Athens) of the "wisdom" of the philosophers of Paul's time, those deemed to be wise by the world. It is parallel to God's odd choice of the weak of the world, those of no account, in order to accomplish "weak" purposes, to shame the strong. God's foolish love of the unlovable, modeled by Jesus' choice of conspicuous sinners for his companions, is the basic theme of this approach.

My own focus has not been on the foolishness or weakness of God, though I rejoice in those images, but rather on the *homelessness* of God. As John D. Caputo writes, "Suppose God most especially pitches his tent among the homeless, so that God has no place to lay his head?"[2]

In this book, as in my life, I want to focus on the homelessness of God as a theme that parallels the weakness and the foolishness of God. My approach to this theme might be considered as a form of *theological graffiti*, working outside accepted theological

1. Bonhoeffer, *Letters and Papers*, 196–197.
2. Caputo, *Weakness of God*, 33.

themes, making unauthorized approaches that are grounded in a crucified Jesus. This is a deliberate attempt to complete a graffiti-like response to those theologians who thrive on discussing the omnipotence, omniscience, and omnipresence of God. This kind of graffiti is somewhat like the fragmentary, provocative nature of Bonhoeffer's letters.

When I speak of doing theology as a kind of graffiti, I follow in what might be called the "wordsteps" of John Caputo. In writing of his weak theology, Caputo describes it as that "which is composed of graffiti that defaces standard theological writing, like a body that is scratched, scarred, and defaced, marred by lines of hunger or persecution, wounded and bleeding. . . . (W)e imagine weak theology as a meditation upon God crossed out, cut and bruised, bleeding and bent in pain. . . ."[3] This explicit comparison of graffiti with the crucified body of Jesus suggests a very different sort of theology is needed, if one begins with a "crossed out" God.

Influenced by the thought of such thinkers as Bonhoeffer and Caputo, I suggest that we speak in our theological graffiti of God's weakness, God's foolishness, and God's homelessness (as distinguished from the ideas of omnipotence, omniscience, and omnipresence).

Language about a "homeless God" does not imply that God is only to be found by homeless people or among homeless people. It *does* imply that God's presence is unpredictable. God is known in surprising times and surprising places. God's presence cannot be controlled or managed. There is no reliable place or context for looking for God. It is not necessarily a fault of humans when God's presence is not experienced. God's absence is part of the mystery of God. Rather than being the fault of humans, the absence of God sometimes becomes an accusation against God, an accusation taken seriously in biblical writings. Speaking of a "homeless God" may help us to recognize God when God is, in fact, present, since such language as "weakness," "foolishness," and "homelessness" *redirects* our attention and our awareness. We would not want to

3. Ibid., 36.

miss the presence of God just because a theology of superlatives blinds us to the humility and homelessness of God.

To speak of the homeless God has moral and political implications. It transforms any hierarchical scale of values. But this has already always been a theme within some strands of Christian thought. Christians place a special value on marginalized people. Christian ethics has what Catholic thought describes as an "option for the poor," a preference for the poor and weak. The impact of Jesus' teaching and example has built this attention to the poor into the basic Christian vision.

My insistence on the homelessness of God is not designed to plead for the special place of the poor in Christian ethics, which is already well argued for by many theologians. Rather, my concern is to shift what we mean by God, by God's presence, and to redefine what we can learn to recognize *when it is right there before us*.

Gillian Rose has pointed out that, according to *Halachah*, Jewish law, the soil of death camps "is cursed not consecrated ground."[4]

The absence of God from *some* places is integral to understanding God's presence in *other* places. To think of God as homeless is to begin to notice such things.

We need to take note of those traits typically involved in human experiences of God's presence. I believe that humans experience God as they are *lured* by a vision of reality beyond themselves. The inner sense of being lured may be felt as a yearning, or even, as St. Augustine wrote, a *restlessness*. The experience of God's presence also seems to involve healing, a healing that is often accompanied by tears. Healing is something that our "being present" to God's presence can help with. We are healed, for instance, when other humans are deeply present to us. We are even more deeply healed when God is present to us. It is an example of "weak power" at work. It needs to be said that many experiences of God seem to also involve anger with God. All of these, being lured, being healed in the midst of tears, and being angry, are typical of biblical

4. Rose, *Love's Work*, 13.

accounts of encounters with God.[5] There are doubtless other typical characteristics of such encounters.

I speak of God's presence as *intermittent, powerless, unexpected,* defined at times by its *absence,* impossible to describe without the radical *fracturing* of language. To speak of homeless presence is to decentralize God's presence. "Homelessness" does for God's *presence* what "weakness" does for God's *status.* This kind of awareness recasts our basic sense of God.

To get at these issues and claims, one needs to stand outside the world of systematic theology or philosophical theology. One needs to be skilled at theological graffiti, standing somewhere to the side of things, writing in a fragmentary way. Early Christians engaged in graffiti by scratching simple fish symbols into Roman walls, alerting others to the *constant presence* of believers, despite the persecution of Christians by the authorities. In that sense, my approach to God is somewhat like that, with God being present in specific places but also being present in many places.

If we move towards this very different theological field of discourse, the question of presence becomes crucial. For instance, in Elie Wiesel's gripping description of the hanging of a young Jewish man in a concentration camp, a death that took thirty minutes to complete, the question that is inevitably asked is, "Then where is God?"[6] This is a very concrete, passionate, tormented theological question. We are no longer thinking abstractly about God. We want to know where God is. The issue is not God's omnipresence; the issue is God's presence.

5. Derrida, *Memoirs of the Blind,* 126–128.
6. Wiesel, *Night,* 60–62.

7 BIBLICAL IMAGES

Jesus pointed out that, though the foxes have holes and birds of the air have nests, he had no place to lay his head (Matthew 8:20). He and his ragged band of followers moved around the country like an itinerate band of thieves, moving from town to town. He was dependent on the hospitality of others. Many of the critical incidents that the tradition remembered occurred in the homes of others, when Jesus benefited from their hospitality. The story of Jesus' birth, as told in the gospel of Luke, seems designed to build on the theme of homelessness, depicting Jesus as born in a stable since "there was no room in the inn" (Luke 2:7). It is said that Jesus was buried in the tomb of a stranger, since he had no place of his own (Luke 23:50–53). If Jesus' lifestyle is a revelation of God, why not push forward with this image of homelessness?

Robert Funk noted that Jesus was a walker. Being a walker is integrally related to being homeless. Indeed, Funk called Jesus a "saunterer." He pointed out that the word contains traces of a deeper, theological meaning. Funk borrowed the insight of another determined walker, Henry David Thoreau. Idlers wandered through Europe in the Middle Ages, begging alms on the pretext of going *a la Sainte-Terre*, to the Holy Land. Children would joke, "There goes a *Sainte-Terrer*," a saunterer. Jesus, of course, traversed Galilee and Judea constantly, offering parables that spoke of ordinary people and common events, parables that evoked the ultimate horizon of God's kingdom, a different sort of holy land.[1]

1. Funk, *Jesus as Precursor.*

33

What might it mean to suggest that Jesus reveals a homeless God, God as Saunterer? It suggests a God who is on the move, seeking out places to be present. If we conceive God as a homeless walker, we're suggesting God as one who moves from place to place. In philosophical terms, it suggests a God *in process*. In biblical terms, God is not described as omnipresent; God's presence is specific and on the move. Jacob can be startled that God "was in this place," something Jacob had not previously realized (Genesis 28:16). God promises an angel will "go before" the people of the Exodus (Exodus 23:23, 32–34). Moses is reassured that "My presence will go with you" (Exodus 33:14). The ark of God, a very specific focus of Yahweh's presence, is moved by David to Jerusalem, as he dances on his own journey alongside it (2 Samuel 6). In Elijah's experience, God was not in the wind, or the earthquake, or the fire. God's presence was in a still, small voice (1 Kings 19:11–12). In the Gospel of John, Jesus even compares the presence of the Spirit with the wind, which "blows where it wills, and you do hear the sound of it, but you do not know whence it comes or whither it goes" (John 3:8).

A classic statement of Hebrew faith begins "A wandering Aramean was my father" (Deuteronomy 26:5). Biblical "ethics" emphasize the need for hospitality to the sojourner, for the people of Israel have been sojourners and, indeed, it is explicitly said that they are strangers and sojourners along with God (Leviticus 25:23).

The point is not to "proof-text" any of these examples, basing everything on one biblical sentence. There are many such instances and each of them would need to be explored in its context. It seems clear, however, that biblical views of God do not focus on an abstract omnipresence. Rather, the *presence* of God is very specific and "on the move." One could perhaps say that God is always present but we are not aware of it. But in religious experience, the presence of God is specific and highly powerful. A lot gets lost if we begin to speak of an abstract or generalized omnipresence.

The earliest Christians celebrated the presence of God *and* the presence of Jesus after his death, sometimes referring to that sense of presence as the Spirit. The first celebration of Pentecost after the crucifixion of Jesus was evidently an extraordinary outpouring of the presence of God and the presence of Jesus, of the spirit of God and the spirit of Jesus. In the early church, "spirit" and "presence" seem to have been interchangeable. Of course, this wonderful celebrative sense became formalized over the years into the doctrine of the Trinity: Father, Son and Holy Spirit. There was something precious, however, about the early free-flowing celebration of God's presence, without ever being extremely careful about precise definitions of spirit and presence.

We also need to recognize that the experience of God includes the "dark night of the soul," the powerful sense of God's absence. Most notably, it includes Jesus' own experience of forsakenness, when he asked "My God, my God, why hast thou forsaken me?" (Luke 15:34).

Human experience of God seems to fluctuate between a sense of God's presence and a sense of the absence of God. Sometimes we pray and seem to be in God's presence; other times we yearn for a God who is not there. God is near to us in the sacraments; at other times they seem like empty forms. A spirit or presence seems to brood over nature; other times nature seems barren, indifferent, or cruel. We can do what Mother Teresa did and spend our lives among the poor and oppressed, hoping that the homeless God will be near us as well as near to the homeless. Yet Mother Teresa's writings tell us more about the absence of God, the desperate yearning for God, than about the presence of God. The presence of God is never guaranteed. Sometimes God is at home in our lives. Many times, probably most times, God is not there. Something like that seems to be the truth about our experience of God.

It is, of course, the "omnis" that do us in. Writers such as Caputo have suggested a God who is a weak force, in distinction from the *omni*potence of the traditional picture. And the "foolishness" of God's love redefines our thought about the *omni*science or wisdom of God. But God has also traditionally been depicted as *omni*present. This depiction seems to come from a theological obsession with superlatives, rather than from human experience or most biblical accounts. Probably the strongest biblical support for omnipresence would be the 139th Psalm:

> Whither shall I go from thy Spirit?
> Or whither shall I flee from thy presence?
> If I ascend to heaven, thou art there!
> If I make my bed in Sheol, thou are there! (Psalm 139: 7–8)

This Psalmist writes here of encountering God wherever he seeks to flee from God. But that is an odd and unique approach to God's omnipresence, not unlike the prophet Jonah's encounter with God when he sought to flee in any direction away from Ninevah. The experience of some people involves encountering God in odd places, even when trying to ignore, neglect, or flee God. More typical of biblical and human experience is the *absence* of God from places where we try to find God. Many people experience God as lacking or absent in their lives, even when they seek God. There are many complex dimensions of experiencing any human "presence," and even more so in experiencing God's presence.

It seems critical to a faithful account of Jesus' vision that God is to be found among weak, marginalized, poor, unclean, hungry, and, indeed, *homeless* people. His God is aligned with the oppressed. The idea of God's presence uniformly distributed throughout all points of space sounds more like some odd theory of physics or astronomy, rather than an attempt to capture the nature of human experience of God. Perhaps the most typical human experience pertaining to God is the absence of God. A sense of God's presence tends to be surprising, rather than the norm. It is how we come to know God in a world of contingencies.

It is difficult enough to talk with precision about *human* presence. Martin Buber, for instance, introduced the idea of "I-Thou" relations into our vocabulary, in order to capture some of the aspects of human presence. We don't really have a vocabulary for talking about God's presence. Our language is built on describing ordinary realities and, even then, the idea of presence tends to be slippery. Applying this to God becomes even more demanding.

God's concern, in the teachings of the Prophets and of Jesus, is with the weak, the sick and dying, the poor, the oppressed, the marginalized, and the homeless. Indeed, God is with those who are so often invisible, living under bridges or hidden away in remote wings of hospitals or nursing homes, refugees, exiles, the hunted, the rejected, immigrants, all those who develop necessary skills at being both there and not there, an invisibility that mirrors the invisibility of God.

8 THE PRESENCE OF GOD

My claim is not that only Christians experience the presence of God, which would be a silly claim. Others may use another vocabulary. God may be present in and described by various vocabularies, including vocabularies lacking the word "God" or similar words. The Jewish tradition of the Shekinah (the divine female presence of God) is very suggestive to me as I ponder these things.[1] Such an exploration would yield results much closer to my position than to claims of traditional omnipresence. Nonetheless, some of us are set free to know the presence of God by reflection on the life of Jesus, especially by meditation on the sauntering, homeless style of Jesus. My point is that God's presence may be known more intensely if we are set free from expecting merely a uniformly omnipresent God.

If we turn from speculation about God's omnipresence to attentiveness to God's presence, we enter a very different field of discourse. Listening to accounts of God's presence is very different from discussing omnipresence. They can be terrifying. It is sometimes as if a tornado has roared through. The language can be raw. I choose as an example an account by Rebecca Ann Parker, an accomplished theologian. But her account of God's presence requires a very different sort of telling and listening.

> When I was raped as a child, there was a moment that I have been able to remember in which I was quite sure I was going to die—and perhaps I was, in fact, close to being killed.

1. Novick, *Wings of Shekinah*.

I was being orally raped. I couldn't breathe. I was just a small child! Four years old. And the weight of the man on top of me was crushing. In that moment I knew that there was a Presence with me that was "stronger" than the rapist and that could encompass my terror. This Presence had a quality of unbounded compassion for me and unbreakable connection to me. . . .

This Presence could not stop the man from killing me, if he chose to. And, at the same time, it *could* stop him. Because, I knew, if he noticed it he *would* be stopped. He would not be able to continue. You couldn't. It was clear to me. You couldn't be aware of this Presence and do what the man was doing to me. He only could do it by not noticing, not knowing. So, this Presence *did* have the power to save me from death and there is a way in which I believe it did. . . .

I know that had he killed me, it would have been because he completely denied the Presence. Such denial is possible and happens all the time.[2]

I am in no position to assess the accuracy of Parker's memory of her four-year-old self. I'm simply pointing to the kind of language that the mature and theologically accomplished Parker is driven to use in speaking of God's presence: a very different world of discourse than when people talk about God's omnipresence.

This description fits within the framework of a God whose presence is known as "luring." If we are attracted towards the good, we are lured. But if there are depths beneath which we cannot sink, then that is still the work of luring, though the restraint placed on our depravity is typically described as an experience of God's "judging." There is Parker's adult experience of healing, the context for her recounting of this story. There is also the presence that, in different ways, played a role in the experience of both the child, who was sustained, and her rapist, who was restrained. Parker writes, "(A)wareness of presence can be fleeting, dimly perceived, jumbled, and intermittent. Violence can fracture this knowing. It

---

2. Brock and Parker, *Proverbs of Ashes*, 211–212.

can destroy the numinous quality of life, as truly as it can place in clear terms the light of presence."[3]

---

3. Ibid., 213.

9 TOUGH QUESTIONS

Rita Charon directs a "medicine and literature" program at Columbia University. A major purpose of this program is to expose medical students to the world of literature, improve their own narrative skills in thinking about their work, and foster their ability to do "close readings" of their own medical narratives, as well as of more traditional literature. Part of this training involves the students in writing "parallel charts," accounts that cover the same medical arena that generates traditional charts, but which use their growing narrative skills to think in different ways about their experience. Charon shares five of these one-page charts, which were based on some experience during the previous week's medical work. They are each very much worth reading, confirming Charon's attempt to enhance both medicine and literature by their interaction. Some are tough to read, moving and disturbing. However, one unusual parallel chart, identified only as "Nell's" chart, seems pertinent to this discussion.

> One day last week, during hour two and a half of rounding, I saw a young man walking down the hospital towards me. The seven of us on my team were standing in a circle, the two interns, the two attendings, the resident and my fellow student; I was the only one facing his direction. He was unassuming, of average height and build, with wavy brown hair, green eyes and glasses. He had no shoes on, only gleaming white socks. He kept trying to catch my eye, like he knew me, as he walked towards us down the hall. He had a mischievous smile on his face.

When he was only two feet from the group, he winked at me. Quickly. Joyously. As if we were in on some great joke together. I don't know if it was my sleep deprivation or the blood rushing from my brain after standing so long, but I thought to myself what if this young man, who seems to want to let me in on his prank, was God? The idea filled me with joy. It was revitalizing. What a strange thought to have! Why would I think that, I asked myself? First, this is exactly where God would want to hang out, in a hospital amongst the sick and the dying and amongst those always around the sick and the dying. And this is exactly how God would want to appear, as a patient, though one inexplicably cheerful in the face of suffering. And why not? He's in on the joke that the rest of us aren't. Finally, God would definitely not want to wear shoes. I can't picture God in shoes.

I was hoping that God would visit some of my patients. Let them in on what was so funny. I hoped he would stop by the room of my 35-year-old patient with CF, now three years older than she ever should have been. God could put on His contact isolation precautions and go in for a chat, put His socked feet up on the windowsill. He could explain why a 35-year-old woman is in the hospital drowning. Why she is the youngest person on the floor by forty years. Why she is counting the rest of her life in months.

After God told that patient His joke, maybe he could move down the hall and look in on another patient of mine. His ALS has left him trapped in a coffin that once was his body, no longer able to eat, to urinate, to move and almost to breathe. Any day and that will be gone too. He can understand though, his mind is still there. He would want to know God's joke. I think he would appreciate it. If it's a good day, my patient might be able to wink back at Him.

And last of all, I hope God comes back my way and lets me in on the secret. Maybe then I can know how to handle pain and sickness on a daily basis, how to welcome death in the second case and accept it in the first. How to sit with suffering, anger and regret without wanting to avoid it and save myself. The secret must be how to sacrifice the idea of justice for peace, how to substitute science for fear.

But God doesn't stop to tell me the joke. Not just yet. He only smiles mysteriously, winks and shuffles off down the hallway.[1]

I was astonished as I first read this account. It has strong traces of irony and anger, as well as humor. It's easy enough to "explain" as a result of sleep deprivation experienced by the young doctor-in-training, the explanation Nell herself considers. But she writes of this as a profound experience, not a passing hallucination. For my purposes, the most important aspect is that I seemed to experience the presence of God in my own act of reading the account. The important question, which I do not probe here, is whether it is possible to experience the presence of God through stories or narratives about God, rather than "directly," as in the accounts of Parker and Nell. Since all I have of Jesus is a narrative *about* Jesus, my implicit claim is that it is also possible to experience God through a narrative. I also believe that many other narratives may also be signs of God.

On the face of it, it is no more absurd to think God was present in Nell's experience than to think God was once present in a wandering young man who healed a few people and told odd stories, a claim millions of people believe today. Some of Nell's questions are the questions I would want to ask of God. Obviously, I like the hint that "(T)his is exactly where God would want to hang out, in a hospital amongst the sick and the dying and amongst those always around the sick and the dying. And this is exactly how God would want to appear, as a patient, though one inexplicably cheerful in the face of suffering. And why not? He's in on the joke that the rest of us aren't. Finally, God would definitely not want to wear shoes. I can't picture God in shoes." This is a wandering God, even a sauntering God, one who obviously would hang out with those who were not able to be in their homes. An account such as this does not fit into the authorized vocabulary for talking about God. It is not an essay about God's omnipresence. Rather, it is a tough

1. Charon, *Narrative Medicine*, 169–170.

account of God's presence, told in a language that is not certified by those who belong to "the club." Moving from a view of God's omnipresence to a search for God's presence opens us to very different kinds of experience. To experience God's presence is not a given; presence is grace.

The presence of God is not merely a sub-category of omnipresence. The intense sense of the presence of God in human experience is not the sort of thing that can be omnipresent. Many models have been borrowed from Jesus' life to describe God. I propose "homelessness" as a relatively unexplored model or metaphor for God. Such a metaphor provides leverage in overcoming the pervasiveness of the idea of God's omnipresence. Using this metaphor presupposes that Jesus' life is not something that disappears as Jesus is exalted or ascends. Jesus' life and teachings are not a temporary illusion, to be waved away in an exaltation. God really is like Jesus as he lived on earth. The sort of language used to describe an experience of the presence of God tends to be raw, blunt, and disturbing. To describe the experience, one gropes for words that are different from talk about the omnipresence of a "greatest conceivable" God. A person could miss the presence of God by being preoccupied with standard academic discourse about God.

What does the presence of God mean for people who are aware of it? Some people, like C. S. Lewis, experience this as Joy. Augustine wrote that our hearts are restless till we find our rest in God. Certainly many people experience a deeply needed forgiveness. Others describe a lure, even a "vision" of God. My own concern is with the presence of God as a source of healing. Some of us don't think of ourselves as evil; we are more likely to think of ourselves as broken. When I try to make myself open to the presence of God, by humming a favorite hymn as I used to hear my father do, or by praying, or by simply being quiet the way Quakers do, what I am trying to be open to is healing.

There is another possible view of God. Describing this view is difficult because there is no single great thinker, no great religion, and no great literature associated with it. Yet it is there, somewhat hidden, at the heart of some thinkers, religions, and literatures.

It is possible to understand God as a permeating, pervasive presence, all around us and within us, yet only occasionally noted by people. It is an unusual experience that some people only occasionally have. It is there to be noticed, but it sometimes seems to disappear when we try too hard to find it. It is a God within whom we live and move and have our being.

This view is somewhat in tune with the understanding of God in process panentheism. That is a view of God as including us and also including all other things. In process theology, we are lured by God, although we are only rarely aware that the lure experienced in our lives might be the lure of God. According to Whitehead and others, we enhance or enrich God; God remembers us. We live our lives within the inclusive life of God.

Process panentheism provides a conceptuality for a view of God as permeating. Yet process panentheism tends to remain a somewhat abstract conceptuality. The view I want to explore here is that, in addition to our being *within* God, God is intimately *around* us. God is *around* us as intimately as the writer of the 139th Psalm experienced God as *within* himself. And God is not only permeating our world, God is indeed within us because of this intimate pervasiveness.

In her book on prayer, Marge Suchocki, herself deeply influenced by process thought, describes this God as having some of the quality of *water*. Suchocki uses water as a metaphor for God, a life-giving substance that is both within us and also all around us. She describes God as pervasive and permeating. She writes of God as water, filling every space, seeking out possible bays, outlining all the physical and spiritual land of our lives, all that for which we have a desperate need. ". . .God is like the rushing water of the universe, filling all spaces, honoring all spaces, centering all spaces through the specialness of divine presence."[2] And she also writes, "God's presence, like water, pervades the nooks and crannies of existence—what is the boundary of water? The boundary of God?"[3] Indeed, prayer is a context in which a person might indeed be-

2. Suchocki, *In God's Presence*, 5.

3. Ibid., 9.

come aware of the permeating God. That is a major reason people pray. And making oneself available for this awareness is a helpful definition of prayer.

However, air can also be a metaphor for this pervasive God. We are surrounded by air, we inhale it, it gives us life. It is pervasive and permeating. It fills in all available space. Hymns, such as the hymn that opens with the words "Breathe on me, Breath of God, fill me with life anew," build on this insight. The word "spirit," frequently used to suggest the presence of God, has overtones suggestive of both air and God.

Jesus of Nazareth seems to have been one of those who experienced God in this pervasive way. Jesus often called God *Abba*, an unusual name for God, even though, in the Aramaic language Jesus most often spoke, it was familiar enough, even an intimate name for human fathers. It is usually translated "Father," as in the phrase "Our Father, who art in heaven." Jesus seems to have lived with a constant awareness of the presence of Abba. He lived with a sense of being surrounded by Abba. Indeed, it is worth noting that when he cried out on the cross, "My God, my God, why has thou forsaken me?" he used a different, more standard name for the God who had seemed to disappear. Jesus is described as calling out for "Eli," a familiar variation on "Elohim," one of the more dominant names for God in Hebrew history.

That passage, in which Jesus cries out asking God why he had been forsaken, is, I believe, the most powerful passage in the New Testament. For one thing, it seems to me that it is likely to be an authentic memory of Jesus' crucifixion. Why would the early church invent a story about Jesus that suggests a breach between the Abba God and Jesus? It also suggests that, for Jesus to suddenly ask why Abba was not present, he must have been very familiar with the constant presence of God. For most of us, I suspect, an intense awareness of God's presence is a rare and treasured experience, rather than a pervasive experience in which we suddenly sense God's absence.

Jesus' parables typically concerned Abba; he would retreat from companions to pray to Abba. There is some problem when

Abba is translated by the word "Father." I am convinced that feminine adjectives are as helpful as masculine terms in describing this pervasive presence. However, the word "Parent" would be so formal, even stiff, that it would lose the intimate sense Jesus suggested by "Abba."

Perhaps the word Abba, familiar enough in Aramaic, is unusual enough to most people to signal a specific understanding of God. Jesus' Abba God notices sparrows (Matthew 10:29–31). There is a touching old song with the line, "His eye is on the sparrow and I know he watches me." Rather than an abstractly omniscient God, Abba seems to be a concretely *noticing* God.

Abba, as a name for God, describes a surrounding, pervasive, supporting, permeating, noticing presence.

Thinking in this way, God might perhaps also be described as porous. A pervasive God finds a way into all kinds of secret places. A porous God would have openings into which other presences might enter. It is tempting to imagine this porous God in a very crude, sponge-like way. This may be the best we can ever do, even as we hold fast in our minds the thought that the openings into the porous God are actually *presences* subtly entering into God's *presence*. I suggest a pervading and even porous God, interacting with our human selves, as we try to define the sensitive inwardness of God.

To explore a *porous* God suggests a different, more immediate sense of things than the God described in typical process panentheistic language. We live our lives in a world deeply known by God, a world pervaded by God, a suffering, knowing, loving place in a porous God.

Perhaps this is the kind of reality behind the "openings" to God so frequently mentioned by George Fox, the great founder of Quakerism. His autobiography often speaks of difficult times, when he was being persecuted and he was struggling for an insight or understanding of a biblical passage. At a crucial juncture, he would experience an "opening" in his understanding. For a while, I thought this was perhaps like a revelation. The root meaning of revelation suggests an "unveiling" of a truth. One problem is that revelation has often been seen as something that can be put into words, a message of some sort. However, Fox already knew the words of the Bible well enough, perhaps better than most of us. Nonetheless, he still struggled. Then would come an opening that let him see scripture, God, and his own life in a new way. Such an "opening" fits into this pattern of pervasive and porous relationships, of human selves and God's own ultimate and inclusive self, defining one another and shaping one another, living lives within the immediate context of one another.

This Quaker imagery is not unlike that of the Shaker communities that developed in England and the United States in the eighteenth and nineteenth centuries. Still well known for their simple, beautiful furniture, music and knowledge of health-creating seeds, the very names of the Shaker and Quaker communities, originally terms of ridicule, suggest the need to physically express a deep involvement with a permeative and porous God. Intense laughter was welcomed in Shaker communities as a sign of a presence. If modern believers are a bit terrified by such extreme motions, we might at least devote some attention to breathing with an awareness of God's presence.

In today's world, the fastest growing Christian communities are Pentecostal communities, deeply defined by the blessings of a Spirit, sometimes resulting in speaking in tongues (glossolalia), healing, weeping, joyful singing, and intense prayer.

All this suggests images of Abba and finite selves permeating one another, open to one another, positing, grounding, and creating one another, in a pattern of deep breathing, dancing, the shaking or quaking of reality, full of weeping and laughing.

Many people who attempt to describe this porous and pervasive God end up using metaphors borrowed from human senses. In his *Confessions*, St. Augustine manages to work in all five senses. "You called and cried out loud and shattered my defenses. You were radiant and resplendent, you put to flight my blindness. You were fragrant, and I drew in my breath and now pant after you. I tasted you, and I feel but hunger and thirst for you. You touched me, and I am set on fire to attain the peace which is yours."[4]

Jesus announced, "Blessed are the pure in heart, for they shall see God." There has been a long tradition of Christians who, inspired by these words, seek the vision of God. There is discussion, of course, as to whether this is a possibility during this life or is reserved for eternal life. Regardless of that issue, the imagery of vision has had a profound impact on understandings of Christian life.[5] Typically, when careful thinkers describe the sensory awareness of God, they say this is achieved by "spiritual senses." Yet, when they describe this awareness, they really have nothing to work with other than metaphors borrowed from the physical senses.

This view of God as a permeating and porous presence is an implicit, even subtle, understanding of God. It describes a God who fills in, hovers, or saturates the empty space defined by our lives. This is a view hinted at by geometrical metaphors. It is driven by attentiveness to what a few communities and persons have said or written about God, especially those influenced by Jesus. Any description of this view is an attempt to breathe in a delicate environment.

I have no idea what God is like a few billion miles from here or what God was like a few billion years ago. Rather than such speculation, we are perhaps better off concentrating on the presence of the present.

This is the point at which it might be helpful to make a comment or two about the world of animal life. Abba seems to be a God of small things, like a woman, Jesus said, searching for a lost coin. In the calculations of the world, a sparrow does not count for much, though the God of Jesus notices the sparrow. I am writing in this book about some of the ways that humans approach or try to understand God. Animals are obviously aware, sentient beings. It is also obvious that animals have a very limited vocabulary for communicating with humans. I do allow myself to ponder at times

4. Augustine, *Confessions*, 201.

5. Kirk, *Vision of God*.

whether some animals nonetheless might have some kind of awareness of God. It seems apparent that elephants weep and do something very much like mourning. Dogs seem to have something
that looks very much like joy. At times they seem to be at peace.
An explorer of consciousness, Christof Koch, writes lovingly of his
German shepherd, watching him carefully in order to ponder the
presence of consciousness. I owe Koch for having introduced me
to a wonderful quotation about dogs from Charles Darwin. "We
have the bark of eagerness, as in the chase; that of anger, as well
as growling; the yelp or howl of despair, as when shut up; the bay-
ing at night; the bark of joy, as when starting on a walk with his
master; and the very distinct one of demand or supplication, as
when wishing for a door or window to be opened."[6] Some criticize
believers for being anthropomorphic in their views of God. I may
sound "animalmorphic" in my questions about animals. I simply
do not want to cut off my own thinking before I know more than
I presently do. I do not know whether or not animals are aware at
times, in a unique way, without a vocabulary, of God.

6. Koch, *Consciousness*, 115–116.

PART III

SIDE WAYS
(ART AND LITERATURE)

10 THE JOY OF
NIGHTMARE ALLEY

A geek is defined in my Random House dictionary as "a carnival performer who performs sensationally morbid or disgusting acts, such as biting off the head of a live chicken." In William Lindsay Gresham's 1947 novel *Nightmare Alley*, we learn that geeks are usually alcoholics who are demeaned enough and desperate enough that they become performers at this lowest level of show business.

I first read Gresham's novel in 1948 as a twelve-year-old boy who enjoyed sneaking books out of my older sister's room. Those books interested me far more than readings assigned in school.

When I noticed that the New York Review of Books had recently republished *Nightmare Alley*, I knew I had to read it again. In fact, the novel stands up remarkably well. It was a best seller at the time, made into a *noir* film with Tyrone Power playing the central figure, Stan Carlisle.

Carlisle begins as a low-level hand in a traveling carnival, a young man getting away from disturbing relationships with his mother and father. He is ambitious and eager to learn and to move on to a different life with more money, power, and women. If all of life is, in essence, a carnival, then that's a good place to begin. Carlisle learns that his boss doesn't *find* a geek, he *makes* a geek by preying on a drunk's fear and desperation. Everyone has a deepest fear and can be controlled if you know that fear. Stan wanders away from this lesson with "the smile of a prisoner who has found a file in a pie."[1]

Carlisle's view of humans becomes ever more dark. He watches the customers who are taken in by the mind-reader Zeena.

> It was the dark alley, all over again. With a light at the end of it. Ever since he was a kid Stan had had the dream. He was running down a dark alley, the buildings vacant and black and menacing on either side. Far down at the end of it a light burned; but there was something behind him, close behind him, getting closer until he woke up trembling and never reached the light. They have it too— a nightmare alley. The North isn't the end. The light will only move further on. And the fear close behind them.[2]

Stan Carlisle masters the techniques of being a "mentalist," moving up from carnivals to the higher ranges of vaudeville. Eventually, he is good enough to move to a much more lucrative level: a spiritualist minister, specializing in the deepest needs of very wealthy people. He has developed a smooth, understanding style that works with desperate people. In this novel, religion is itself a hoax, a manipulative game.

Carlisle becomes ever more influential and successful. He is able to afford nice clothes and expensive brandy. After using a number of women, he himself comes under the control of a psychotherapist with the interesting name of Lilith (Eve's competitor for the job of the first woman in mythology). Carlisle's own life ends up as the fulfillment of his nightmare.

The book is well written, experimenting with a variety of writing styles. It is obviously influenced by the many approaches and literary experiments of James Joyce. One chapter has long, run-on sentences, with one sentence being 341 words long. Though not Proustian or Joycian in literary value, it is a controlled, interesting, vivid, and relevant sentence.[3] However, the most interesting literary aspect of the book is its structure. Rather than traditional

1. Gresham, *Nightmare Alley*, 7.
2. Ibid., 67.
3. Ibid., 173.

chapters, each section is named after a card in a tarot deck. The 22 card tarot deck goes back to at least the sixteenth century, with many mysterious themes on its face cards. A chapter might be named "Card XII / The Star / shines down upon a naked girl who, between land and sea, pours mysterious waters from her urns."[4] This description is accompanied by a drawn sketch of the illustration on the face of a tarot card, laden with symbols. One cannot resist the temptation, after reading a "chapter," to turn back to the first page of the chapter to see how the ongoing story of Stan Carlisle relates to the cryptic card.

Carlyle learns of the tarot deck from the mind reader Zeena, who tells him there is good money to be made from the deck. It is possible to weave a story from a sample of these cards that fits the deepest needs (and deepest fears) of the sucker. One wonders, of course, how Gresham is using these cards in the structure of his book. Is the reader the sucker? Or is he suggesting there is some deep pattern in these centuries-old cards? The mood that prevails is that there is some inevitability in human life, as we each play out a script that involves recurrent issues suggested by the cards. The novel certainly does not focus on human freedom and good decision making. We are all marks in a carnival.

Gresham had his own serious drinking problem. Indeed, Nick Tosches suggests, in his Introduction to the new edition, that Gresham's writing must have been "binge-riddled." I find that hard to believe, since the book, in both style and content, is intricate and controlled. There must have been a window of lucidity that resulted in the book.

In 1951, Gresham wrote a statement of his own Christian faith in a volume called *These Found the Way*. It is a collection of essays by thirteen well-known people, all of them intellectuals of one sort or another. Gresham described his early involvement in Marxist youth groups, an outlet for an early desire to make the world a better place. Like many concerned people of his era, he had spent time in Spain, during its civil war. Gradually, as he describes it, he lost his faith in Marxism, having thought about "the

4. Ibid., 165.

double mystery of time and his own consciousness."[5] He presents his story as a move "from communism to Christianity," a logical progression from the false logic of Marxism to the valid logic of Christianity. He also suggests inevitability in his development. Something "happened which is, I think, more important to the Christian than his own search for God. God sought me."[6]

For readers of the novel, one interesting comment in Gresham's essay on his faith refers to one card in the tarot deck. "It is called 'The Hanged Man.' A youth is suspended by one foot from a T-shaped cross. His hands are bound behind his back. He hangs upside down, but on his face is an expression of unearthly peace; from his head radiate spokes of light. And the cross is putting forth shoots of green—living wood, in the spring of the year. The card fascinated me. Slowly, without realizing it, I was coming toward Christ."[7]

"The Hanged Man" is also the final card or chapter in *Nightmare Alley*, but with a much different mood or theme. In that context, the card describes the outcome of Stan Carlisle's own journey, in which he is the one self-destructing, ending up as a geek.

In his essay, Gresham says he had become worried about his drinking in 1948 (two years after the publication of *Nightmare Alley*, which he refers to as "savage, violent, and neurotic, which made money"). At the time of his writing the essay, he says he had not been drinking for seventeen months.

Two central figures are mentioned in his account. Gresham had divorced and married Joy Davidman, a poet and novelist. They had met in their Marxist groups and activities, gradually falling in love. They were both on a spiritual journey and were now active in a small Presbyterian church. Gresham also speaks very highly of the writings of C. S. Lewis; "his vision illumined the Mystery which lay behind the appearances of daily life."[8]

---

5. Soper, *These Found the Way*, 30.

6. Ibid., 80.

7. Ibid., 75.

8. Ibid., 77.

Joy Davidman is also one of the 13 people who recount their faith journeys in this book. She had been the daughter of skeptical Jews. She had been involved as a volunteer in the war in Spain, as had Gresham. She gradually lost her Marxist faith and was led into the Christian faith by the writings of C. S. Lewis. Her experience was similar to Gresham's journey, in that both had to think their ways out of their atheism, getting free of their Marxism and materialism. However, Davidman reports a more intense experience of God than Gresham recounts. "There was a Person with me in the room, directly present to my consciousness—a Person so real that all my previous life was by comparison mere shadow play." She says this intense perception lasted perhaps half a minute.[9] Her life changed. She reports herself as very happy in the same Presbyterian church in Duchess County, New York, that she shared with Gresham and their children.

She mentions Francis Thompson's description of God as the "Hound of Heaven." She describes her own experience of God as more like a cat. God had stalked her for a long time, but very silently. "Then, all at once, he sprang."[10]

Many readers will know the next piece of this account. I will summarize it briefly. Gresham returned to alcohol. Davidman left Gresham in 1953 for C. S. Lewis (two years after their accounts of personal faith had appeared in print). In 1962, Gresham checked into a hotel room and ended his own life. His description of his seventeen sober months and his newly found faith seems in retrospect to have been overly confident. Twelve step programs teach a person to never describe alcoholism as a thing of the past. At best, one can only be a "recovering" alcoholic. Life should be lived "one day at a time." Perhaps the same is true of religious faith. Gresham's life follows a pattern similar to his account of Stan Carlisle's life.

There have been many books about C. S. Lewis and some accounts of his life with Davidman. The best of those books is Brian Sibley's *Through the Shadowlands: The Love Story of C. S. Lewis and Joy Davidman*. A movie *Shadowlands*, based on this account,

9. Ibid., 23.
10. Ibid., 23.

starred Anthony Hopkins and Debra Winger. Davidman died of cancer in 1960; I believe that Lewis' account of his own deep response to her death, *A Grief Observed*, is the best of his books.

Lewis' work is far more highly regarded in the United States than in England. He has become something of an icon to American evangelical Christians. His writing is often highly praised, just as Gresham and Davidman had praised it.

In *Surprised by Joy*, his best-known book, Lewis comes across as very much the Oxford don. He goes on at some length about English writers of his and some earlier generations, such men as Owen Barfield, George MacDonald, and F. K. Chesterton. For Americans today, these names sound vaguely quaint. One has heard of them, but we have not read them with the care and respect Lewis devoted to them. Lewis describes his own preoccupation with the imagination, as earlier Romantics had described it. He describes some early experiences of joy. He gradually shifts to a capital letter for joy, so that an experience of Joy sounds as if it is actually Something. A reader who knows the story of Joy Davidman cannot resist wondering what is in a name.

His discussion of God is put forward as an attempt to avoid God. Instead of a deck of tarot cards, Lewis uses the image of a chess game. There are chapters called Check and, eventually, Checkmate. Lewis is trapped. His mood is not unlike the inevitability of Carlisle's tarot cards, even though his thought is more similar to Francis Thompson's "hound of heaven" approach. He has no choice but to believe in God. Even then, he gradually has to work towards a specifically Christian understanding of God. He sometimes sounds grouchy about the whole thing. At times, that is funny, as when he says that one drawback to becoming a church-going Christian is that one so often has to listen to organ music.

It is not clear to me what Lewis' point is, even though he seems to belong to that group of believers who try to describe some sense of the numinous or the transcendent. For Lewis, it is Joy that gives him a sense of the transcendence. Others have tried in similar ways to define wonder, awe, beauty, or forgiveness.

Lewis does attempt to approach the demonic. His popular book *The Screwtape Letters* details the intimate thoughts of Wormwood, a high-ranking devil. It is a clever, often funny book. It suggests that one can believe in the reality of evil or of Satan, without being primitive or medieval about it. It is implied that it is sophisticated to believe in Satan, especially if one is lighthearted about it. This is a book published in 1955, ten years after the world first began to understand the awful reality of the Holocaust. Yet Lewis suggests that part of the craftiness of Satan is his ability to distract a person from worship by the squeaking shoes of a fellow worshipper.

Lewis' book *Surprised By Joy* is about joy (or Joy). Gresham's novel is about life as an alley of nightmares. *Nightmare Alley* is a tough read, but it has the value of recognizing that we all have demons.

11 SEEK MY FACE

GOD AND PIGMENT

Humans try to create meaning in life and also strive to preserve what is most meaningful to them. Some want to have children, for the sheer joy of children, but also in order to conserve something of their genes. Others produce art or, at least, take photographs of special moments. Wealthy people often like to have their names on buildings, foundations, and endowments. People make wills, to extend their own will into times beyond death. In the past, some people had statues of themselves standing in public places. In more recent times, Maya Lin's Vietnam War memorial in Washington, D.C. has shifted the mood of how we want to memorialize and, somehow, preserve or conserve some human meaning.

And, though I love the process of reading the thoughts of others, contemplating those thoughts and arranging them with some of my own thought, and then writing about all those thoughts, I have to confess that I also enjoy seeing my own name on those writings. I suspect I am not the only scholar who enjoys that very modest conservation of our own value or meaning.

The twentieth-century philosopher Charles Hartshorne wrote about what he sometimes called the "conservation of value." He had in mind something like what I call the preservation (or conservation) of meaning. Hartshorne suggested that religious thinkers tended to focus on the "creation of value" (by way of a creative God), while neglecting the "conservation of value." In Hartshorne's view, God created value by "luring" everything from the microscopic events of deepest reality to the profoundest visions of human lives. He also argued that all this would be meaningless if God did not also conserve that value. Creation and conservation were, in this view, polar aspects of God's relation to the world. God creates constantly by luring. God conserves all things through perfect memory. Our own human lives both *enrich* the fullness of God's life and, sometimes, *cause* God's suffering by our own evil or by our own pain.

In Hartshorne's views, God conserves the value of each event in the ongoing universe by remembering it with a perfect memory. Nothing is lost because God remembers all. We will be remembered by God, both enriching God and contributing to the suffering of God. Many of us would like to be remembered, perhaps by a generation or two of descendants and friends, perhaps even by strangers who know of us. God offers a much more detailed and inclusive memory of us. The purpose of our lives, in the long run, is to enrich God.

This view of God as remembering with ultimate detail and love is sometimes described as "objective immortality." In contrast with more familiar views, which are versions of "subjective immortality" or continuation of subjectivity beyond death, this view saves each moment of life *as it was lived*.

In this vision, objective immortality overcomes what has been described as the "perpetual perishing" of each moment of all lives and all events by their disappearance into the past. As time flows through our lives or, perhaps, as our lives move through time, moments in our lives disappear into the past, sometimes remembered, mostly forgotten. Our lives perish into the past and all around us perishes, sometimes visibly, sometimes seemingly more slowly.

Since being immersed in Hartshorne's thought early in my own life, I have noticed the ways in which I try to create and conserve meaning, the ways other people do so, and the ways that an attempt to conserve meaning can show up in art. Most often, I have noticed the ways that novelists assume that the conservation of meaning is crucial to human life. The writer John Updike often had the conservation of value and meaning as a central theme.

In his four volumes of the Rabbit Angstrom series, Updike covers four decades of Angstrom's life, with the first volume introducing Rabbit in his early twenties, then continuing, approximately every ten years, through the rest of Rabbit's life, till he dies, suddenly, of a heart attack. The series provides a picture of American life through those decades, as well as an intimate account of a fictional, but also typical, American life. The first volume shows Rabbit as already nostalgic for his life as a teenage basketball star. Through remaining volumes, Rabbit ages, ponders some issues of the past catching up with him and the future both luring him and threatening him with death. Time is a constant factor.

I want to focus here on one often overlooked novel from Updike: *Seek My Face.* The book records one day in the life of Hope Chafetz, born Ouderkirk (suggesting "outside the church"), as she is being interviewed by Kathryn D'Angelo, a young cyber-journalist. The interview is prompted by the fact that this aging woman is continuing her own career as a painter, as well as the fact that two of her three marriages were to major artists: the first to an artist remarkably like Jackson Pollock, the second suggestive of several mid-century artists, including Andy Warhol.

It is treacherous to try to establish a novel's "mood," but I think Hope (her name itself offers a clue) sees life as having been well worth living and continues to be stunned by the beauty of things. She is certainly aware of all the signs that she is nearing the end of her life, but she is far more life-obsessed than death-obsessed. It interests me that Updike strikes this affirmative mood when he turns to art as a central interest. It is perhaps pertinent that, as a young man, Updike attended the Ruskin School of Drawing and Fine Art. For Updike, art (and its cousins, color and beauty) provide a way of seeking God's face that "hymns life," as he once put it.

Indeed, Hope's attitude is identical with Updike's own view as expressed in his collection of essays on art, *Just Looking*. Updike writes of his lifelong interaction with New York City's Museum of Modern Art. "But it was among the older and least 'modern' works in the museum that I found most comfort, and the message I needed: that even though God and human majesty, as represented in the icons and triptychs and tedious canvases of older museums, had evaporated, beauty was still left, beauty amid our ruins, a beauty curiously pure, a blank uncaused beauty that signified only itself."[1]

Like many of Updike's most interesting characters, Hope both believes and doesn't believe in God. Indeed, Kathryn begins her interview by citing something Hope had said years earlier in another interview: "For a long time I have lived as a recluse, fearing the many evidences of God's non-existence with which the world abounds." Yet Hope is also convinced by an artist, perhaps modeled after Hans Hofmann, who "had us believing that to make art was the highest and purest of human activities, the closest approach to God, the God who creates Himself in this push and pull of colors."[2] Whatever Updike's own position might be, it is daring to even entertain the thought that God might be self-creating in the push and pull of colors.

Reviewers tended to overlook the centrality of God in *Seek My Face*, despite the fact that Updike quotes Psalm 27 as one of three prefatory quotes: "You speak in my heart and say, 'Seek My Face.' Your face, Lord, will I seek." Updike's two other prefatory quotes strengthen the case for a theological reading of the book, referring to Czeslaw Milosz's thought that visible beauty "is a little mirror for the beauty of being," and Karl Shapiro's suggestion that paint might be gorgeous "and, I hope, holy."

As with so many of Updike's characters, Hope is torn between faith and unfaith, between Nothing and God. She tells Kathryn that art "has to be about us, just a skin away from being nothing. Not nothing perhaps, I don't know what your religion is, but

1. Updike, *Just Looking*, 9.
2. Updike, *Seek My Face*, 38.

tumbling back into the radiance."[3] It's not merely a struggle between Nothing and God, but also between darkness and radiance. All we have are clues, and, for Hope and some others, art offers as good a clue as we are going to get.

It is helpful to follow one specific theme: Updike's use of the image of "hardening." Updike's real concern, and Hope's real passion, is a very creative hardening, the hardening of oil-based paint, the very essence of the art to which Hope has devoted her life.

Even as a child looking at paintings in her grandfather's house, Hope senses the mystery. Updike introduces the theme early in the book.

> The paint *hardened*, Hope saw, touching (the child was alone in the room, there was nobody to tell her not to touch) its little rough spines. The hardened paint carried a glimpse forward into a radiant forever, along with the groping, stabbing movement of the painter's hand and eye. She felt an infinite, widening magic in this, and also the element of protest which made people want to nail down pieces of a world that was always sliding away from under them; the world was an assembly line that kept spilling goods forward, into a heap of the lost and forgotten. With the protest came a gaiety, that of small defiant victories over time, creating *things to keep*.[4]

With the perception that Updike attributes to Hope as a child, the hardening of paint poses the ultimate question of life. Life seems to move inevitably forward, spilling into "a heap of the lost and forgotten." We grope for some meaning that will endure, for some creation that can be *kept*. The fact that paint hardens is one of the few "small defiant victories over time" that suggests a "radiant forever," an "infinite, widening magic." The sense of a "radiant forever" is similar to the hope, quoted above, that perhaps we tumble back into the radiance, instead of into nothing. It is this tension—between the inevitable perishing of life and meaning and

3. Ibid., 25.
4. Ibid., 24.

the hope for a deeper meaning that doesn't perish—which runs throughout this book as, indeed, it does others of Updike's works.

Later, as an adult immersed in the world of art, Hope listens to male artists debate the significance of their work and the eccentricities of paint. "*It hardens*, Hope thought. None of this would be important if paint didn't harden."[5] On the other hand, remembering another painter in their circle who thinned his paint way down, Hope ponders the fact that "curators say they're desperately unstable, which could have been part of his intention: *vita brevis, ars brevis* too."[6]

Reflecting on her Jackson Pollock-like husband Zack, Hope thinks, "He was after eternity. In his mind he was like a Renaissance muralist, working for forever. Permanence was the very thing that the new artists couldn't abide."[7] Zack even allowed accidents to be preserved forever, "like one of the bumblebees he painted into his own drips; the paint hardened and the bee's furry dry body was there forever, mummified."[8] Hope saw herself as a collaborator with Zack, as they "ripped those imperishable hours from the perishing world."[9]

Certainly Hope has a need for something that would endure. "I wanted *paint*, paint that came out gooey and then hardened and couldn't be pushed around any more. That was my idea of art."[10] She is disturbed that the painting of Piero della Francesca is almost all restorer by now and *The Last Supper* is "just a few glued-on crumbs in an empty room in Milan."[11] Hope knows that "all the excuses for art are flimsy and fade; what endures is the art itself, the paint keeping intact whatever hope or intention worked for that perilous moment."[12]

5. Ibid., 50.

6. Ibid., 97–98.

7. Ibid., 233.

8. Ibid.. 118.

9. Ibid.. 214.

10. Ibid.. 185.

11. Ibid.. 233.

12. Ibid., 266.

After I had published an article discussing Updike's use of the metaphor of hardening as an approach to the conservation of meaning, he sent me a postcard. "I think you read me very well, and I'm glad somebody noticed the hardening, the hope of permanence. Same thing, of course, with words hardening into type and not quite the same thing for a musician's performance hardening into wax. We all want to make a mark, as they used to say."

Perhaps wax is not how we preserve beautiful music anymore, but the conservation of that music is still important.

Humans hunger for the conservation, somehow or other, of the meaning of their lives. We try in various ways to conserve that meaning, to not let it dissipate. Yet we don't see how "our love is here to stay," as an old song claims. A perfect ultimate memory would perhaps do it. Perhaps that is what is going on in this moment: it is all being remembered. Or held in God's love. But we don't know. We seek God's face: a radiance that we can only *seek*.

12 ART

VERMEER, DA VINCI, CARAVAGGIO, AND ROTHKO

In 1986, my wife Nancy and I took a vacation trip to England. In London, we wandered into the National Gallery, next to the Green. At the admissions desk, I picked up a sheet of paper claiming to list and give directions to the twenty greatest works of art in the Gallery's collection. Like other tourists, we decided that would be the most "efficient" way to make sure we didn't miss anything, so we found our way to each of the superstars. It was during that afternoon that I realized that I didn't know anything about what I was doing. I had no idea why those twenty paintings were superior to the thousands of other works of art in the collection. Maybe they weren't. Since that day, art has been a central interest and focus of my life. It has also been a good excuse to travel through the United States, Europe, and Japan. I haven't golfed since I retired. In this section I want to discuss the work of four artists who have been important to me: Johannes Vermeer, Leonardo da Vinci, Michaelangelo Caravaggio, and Mark Rothko.

In the paintings of Johannes Vermeer, there is a precision at work that also nonetheless suggests something ultimate. We know that precision was important to Vermeer. Evidence suggests, for instance, that he was one of the first to experiment with a "camera obscura" to assure that his proportions and perspective were correct. This is not to say that he sought photographic accuracy. He composed; he made decisions; he obscured at times; he created a mood. Yet his paintings are precise in ways that paintings of many other artists are not.

Many of Vermeer's paintings belong to a class known as genre paintings. This was far from the highest-ranking category. Unlike paintings from mythology or religious scenes or events of state and history, genre paintings were of domestic interior scenes: ordinary life in private homes. Yet in the hundred or so years since the work of Vermeer has moved back to center stage, it is clear that something more than domesticity is going on. Something is at work in his paintings, some mood of mystery.

My suggestion is that they are paintings of human interiority. Here the scene is one of quiet domesticity. A wall or a window is the only horizon we have. Everything is human-size. Nothing is overwhelming. There is no explicit religious iconography. Yet a presence is felt that, for some of us, hints at the ultimate. Many of his paintings illustrate this. I will focus on "Lady Writing a Letter with Her Maid." This is a painting of a woman writing a letter and of her servant staring out the window. But it's more than that. We sense we are in the presence of two human minds, two spirits. The maid looks out the window, lost in thought. What do we stare at when we stare off into space? Most often, when I "come to myself," I don't know what I have been thinking about. I imagine that often, when I have stared into space, I have been staring into the ultimate. The lady with the pen in her hand is much more focused. She is searching for the right words. But there is also inwardness there: a very precise depiction of how human bodies look when their interiors are alive and well. And once we are in the presence of interiors, we can soon be in the presence of ultimacy.

The fact that a precise description of the world in art or language can evoke ultimacy is important. Ultimacy is not a concept or awareness that only arises with the unusual or extraordinary. Simply being attentive to the everyday world as it actually exists can raise the issue of ultimacy. There is something about the world precisely described that, if one is not anesthetized by the ordinary and the daily, evokes its own wonder in contemplation of the ultimate. The ordinary world, precisely described, includes people lost in thought, staring out the window into empty space.

Interestingly, Vermeer also has two paintings, usually called "The Geographer" and "The Astronomer," of men literally staring into space, surrounded by the paraphernalia of their scientific trades. They may be staring at a globe, in one case, and out a window, in another, but they clearly are filled with wonder as they also stare into infinity. The implicit reality of the emerging worldview suggested by science is clear in paintings depicting astronomy and geography. But, again, there is the thoughtfulness, the musing, of the two men, suggesting a world of consciousness containing universes within itself.

Many great painters, including Giotto, del Sarto, Titian, Rubens, and Tiepolo have painted Jesus' last supper with his disciples. I will comment on the paintings of two: Leonardo da Vinci from the Italian Renaissance and Michaelangelo Caravaggio from the Baroque period. I have traveled to see both of them.

Leonardo da Vinci's depiction of the last supper, painted on the wall in a monastery's refectory in Milan, is certainly the best known of the various depictions of the subject. To actually stand before it today is to see pale flakes of paint. It is gradually fading out of existence. The best reason to go is to see its context. The room that served as a place for the monks to gather for meals is now a place to see the painting. The light is turned on for a few moments, then turned off to limit the erosion of the painting.

In Leonardo da Vinci's painting, there is an invisible, dominating presence. It is not the Holy Spirit. Rather, it is Renaissance perspective. This mural is primarily a display of the power of perspective, with Jesus having twelve disciples sitting six on each side. Jesus himself is the axis pointing to the vanishing point. All the lines in the mural, of table, ceiling beams, floor, etc., merge, in their implied extensions, on Jesus' head. Jesus' head is the vanishing point. Jesus therefore is both the visual center of the painting and the point from which an infinite regress into the virtual depth of the painting is implied. The insight comes when you realize that the lines of the room in which you are standing (the old refectory) has its own lines leading along the ceiling and the floor directly into the lines of the fading painting. That is how the monks could see the painting as they ate.

There are so many lines in the mural itself reinforcing the point that this particular painting is a mathematically precise example of what Renaissance painting was trying to do. Da Vinci was a master of perspective. The lines are sharp and clearly edged, even if they are fading and flaking away. Though the scene has certain oddities (everyone sitting on one side of the table, the dog), the basic style is one of realistically capturing how people at a table might look. But there is also a worldview contained in the use of perspective. This painting announces itself as a "modern" painting, one aligned with the new vision of the cosmos: mathematically precise, knowing there are many perspectives, knowing that vision penetrates towards an infinite depth, a horizon unlike what was envisioned only a couple of centuries earlier. It is both precise and aware that there are many centers with no circumference.

The painter known as Caravaggio left a very different depiction of the last supper, when compared with da Vinci's effort. This is a depiction of a post-resurrection meal, with two disciples who encountered the risen Christ on the road to Emmaus. The figures are very different. Instead of the ethereal figures of da Vinci, the figures in Caravaggio's painting are unmistakably male. They are muscular, blunt featured, weighty, earthy beings. They are depicted much closer to the painting's surface than in da Vinci's painting, where the figures are securely behind a table, seen in its entirety. Caravaggio's table is only partially depicted as it fills the picture plane.

Most importantly, there is no Renaissance perspective in this last supper by Caravaggio. There is no depth at all, only a bland, dark background. Caravaggio creates perspective in a very different way, by having the figures gesture outwards into the viewer's space. A disciple's shoulder and Jesus' hand come out of the picture. This is truly an "in your face" painting. This is not an expansion back to a vanishing point, into infinity. This is a transgression of boundaries, a pulling of the viewer into the action. It doesn't reach into infinity. It is right here. Caravaggio creates a sort of "real presence" in this depiction of Jesus' supper. It reaches into the viewer's space, just as Jesus' parables do. It does not suggest an infinity of depth; it strives rather for a disturbing intimacy.

Simon Schama puts it well.

> Caravaggio is the most confrontational of painters, with everything calculated to be too close for comfort. His big paintings get in our face like no others because they are designed to rip away the protective distance conferred by high art. A blaze of light catches the figures, but around them is utter blackness swallowing up the comfort zone of art-gazing: frame, wall, altar, gallery. The great break-through of Renaissance painting had been perspective, the depth punched through the far side of the picture plane. But Caravaggio is more interested in where *we* are. In the space in front of the picture plane which he makes a point of invading. Looking at the outflung arms of Christ in his *Supper at Emmaus*. . . you almost duck to avoid the impact. Caravaggio isn't a beckoner—he's a grabber, a button-holer; his paintings shamelessly come out and accost us, as if he were crossing the street and, oh God, coming our way. "You *looking* at me?"[1]

Graham Dixon points out that the artist Caravaggio "painted *as if* the rich and the powerful were his enemies, *as if* he really did believe that the meek deserved to inherit the earth."[2] This is painting with "a slant."

In his mature paintings, Mark Rothko painted on a primarily vertical canvas. Typically, he painted two or three bars of color across the canvas. The bars usually have blurred edges that fade into the background. If one simply sits in front of a Rothko (he liked his canvases hung low with benches that met his specifications in front of them), one should be close enough to not wonder where the horizon might be. One experiences a profound sense of being drawn into Rothko's paintings. There is no illusion that one is looking at anything other than bars of color on a canvas. They

1. Schama, *Power of Art*, 18.
2. Dixon, *Caravaggio*, 438. My italics.

are, however, marvelous colors. Rothko painted with thin washes of color, so there seem to be depths of color behind the surface "teasing the eye into a lit core of indeterminate depth."[3] The colors shimmer and dance, "doing a steady throb, like the valve of a body part."[4] Until his last, very somber work, the colors are joyous and unlike anything seen before, as they play off one another. I need to sit before his canvases for some time before I begin to experience their effect. Rothko liked canvases large enough that they were bigger than the humans viewing them, so that one could become lost in them. I usually experience a sense of vertigo before I begin to drown in the painting. This is the painting of ultimate immanence, of being swallowed whole by the colors as they surge before your eyes, a pantheistic ultimacy that is engulfing the viewer. As Simon Schama puts it, one might at first think of Rothko's paintings as forbidding. "But in fact they are embracing."[5]

Mark Rothko's last great work was for a chapel designed for Everyman, or Everyone. The Menil Chapel in Houston has no sectarian apparatus. There are simply the large dark canvases, mostly black, broken only by hints of purple. Rothko always had a tragic sense of life and worried that the colors of his earlier work were too pretty, that people bought his painting without realizing that he was up to something monumental. There can be no doubt that the Menil Chapel setting is tragic. James Elkins has suggested there has been more weeping before Rothko's chapel paintings than before any other works of art.[6] One can analyze the texture of the paint for some variety, but the color mood is unfailingly somber, dark, tragic: black with a hint of purple. Some writers seek to analyze the cosmic vision in the chapel by the relationships between the panels, the axis of the room, and the loneliness or relatedness of the panels.[7] However, it seems clear that Rothko has painted not

3. Schama, *Power of Art*, 418, 422.

4. Ibid., 400.

5. Ibid., 437.

6. Elkins, *Pictures and Tears*, 2.

7. Nodelman, *Rothko Chapel Paintings*.

simply the ground of the cosmos, but also the abyss that always seems ready to swallow the ground.

PART IV

GOD FOR AN OLD MAN

13 DYING

AN INTERIM REPORT

In April of 2006, I was diagnosed with lymphoma, a cancer of the blood. I began immediately to receive intensive chemotherapy. I was told that I had months or perhaps a year to live. That summer I began to put some of my thoughts into words. That essay was published later in the journal Soundings. *The rest of this chapter is taken from that article.*

It's an odd place to be. I feel fine; I am alert; I enjoy life immensely. Yet I also know that my lymphoma is treacherous and that I am likely to die from it "within years or in months," as my oncologist puts it.

I was diagnosed less than two months ago, as I write. As I was promised, my disease is "treatable." The original symptoms have about all cleared up and the chemotherapy itself is not really that bad to deal with. However, even if my condition is treatable, it is not "curable," in the carefully chosen words I have learned to use. The cancer is highly likely to return and the chemicals that have given me the upper hand for a while will be less effective as they are used again.

So, it's an odd place to be. To feel as if I am fine, but to know that the only way not to lose this battle is to die from something else first. It's time to assess things in the way that I am accustomed to assessing them. I am a humanist, immersed in philosophy, theology, literature and art, rather than a scientist. How am I doing?

I notice that I have become more organized, wanting to arrange things, to get things in order. I've always had trouble throwing things away. I have a large cardboard box full of old socks with holes in them. I've saved them on the basis that if I ever need to paint or stain something, they would be handy to wear. Of course, I almost never paint anything and, even though I stain the deck on our house every couple of years, there are many more socks by far than I could ever use.

Therefore I have begun to throw away old clothes; I sort through stacks of old letters; I arrange my desk. Some of this, of course, is a chance to go back over my past, to ponder the handwriting of my parents from decades ago. There are old photos and even an old dispute over a bill.

I've always worked with a cluttered desk, with stacks piled all around me as I scan the singular clarity and neatness of my computer screen. Now I'm going through those stacks, throwing away many things, sorting other things into newly defined stacks, writing notations on manila files.

In one of those stacks, I came across an index card the other day, with four phrases written on it.

> Denial of death
> Denial of self
> Denial of the past
> Denial of meaning

I knew this was a note to myself from a couple of years ago, from pre-lymphoma days, a listing of some ideas that seemed to me to be connected to one another. I knew that I thought that people, in their religions and philosophies, tend to deny one or more of these four things: death, the self, the past, and meaning. I also knew that I wanted to deny these denials, to insist on the reality of death, the self, the past, and meaning.

Of course, the denial of death is deep in human nature. My choice of the term "denial" to describe the ways that people handle death, as well as other things, was almost certainly borrowed from Ernest Becker's classic book *The Denial of Death*. It's not as if the person with a terminal illness has somehow lost a lottery that other people have managed to win. It's a lottery in which there are no winners, but the proof of that hits people in the stomach at different times.

I believe in God and I call myself a Christian. I have spent a lot of time thinking about the various religious views that people draw on to deny death: reincarnation and immortality of the soul and resurrection of the body. Probably resurrection of the body is the view that I find most interesting and that comes closest to some kind of credibility. I have spent a lot of time over the years reading about and thinking about the relation of mind and body. Mind and body seem so deeply enmeshed in one another that I really can't picture a soul or mind enjoying personal immortality or reincarnation in some unrelated body. From an intellectual perspective, resurrection of my body by God's grace into another realm seems well within God's capabilities.

But I don't really think it will happen. My reasons for my skepticism are not especially sophisticated. For one thing, I just don't have any interest in ongoing existence in some other realm. It's this earthly realm, the only arena I know, that interests me. I watch baseball players point towards the heavens after hitting a home run, acknowledging a mother or some other loved one who is looking down. I quietly listen to someone say at a wedding or graduation that he or she "knows" that some loved one is watching the whole thing from heaven. All of this simply confirms me in the view that the real action is right here on earth. All those people with a far more sure and simple faith than I have can't imagine their loved ones with anything more interesting to do than watching events unfold on earth. I can't either. John Updike (inspired by Unamuno) put it best for me when he wrote, ". . .the basic desire, as Unamuno says in his *Tragic Sense of Life*, is not for some other world but for this world, for life more or less as we know it to go on forever: 'The immortality that we crave is a phenomenal immortality—it is the continuation of this present life.'[1] My other problem with any continuing life after death is more theological. If the purpose of life here on earth is to prepare us morally or spiritually for another life, it strikes me as an odd arrangement. The ways in which we grow spiritually or build character seem unrelated to any purpose in some other life. If God's real purpose for us is another world, then why not create a more efficient way of getting us into that other world? D. Z. Phillips writes, "When all is said and done, our story is offered another, of a world to come, occupied by creatures who are not human beings. Then I would ask, What do they know about us?"[2]

So, in the last analysis, it is boredom with the thought of some life after my death in *this* life that finally determines my thoughts about the possibility of such a life. It would be marginally possible to come up with some kind of intellectual defense of a continuing life; it simply doesn't interest me.

I have spent more energy on worldviews that deny the self. There are many reasons to question the reality of a continuing self, but I'm aware that one of my motivations in exploring the theme has been as a way of dealing with pain and death. With its doctrine of No Self, Buddhism is the best example of a religious philosophy that denies the self. Buddhism exists as a way of overcoming human suffering; a critical factor in suffering is the deception that the self exists and endures. We are constantly changing in our thoughts, senses, emotions, bodies, and dispositions, those basic states of being or *skandhas* that create the illusion of substance and continuity. The self is simply the constellation that all these factors form at any given moment. The next moment, a different constellation takes form. There is no need to be anxious about the fate of the self, since the self as we know it won't exist in the future. By realizing that there is No Self, we no longer need to ride the highs and lows of the roller coaster. We simply get off the roller coaster.

1. Updike, *Self-Consciousness*, 217.
2. Phillips, *Problem of Evil*, 90.

Most religions teach the need to overcome the Ego, but Buddhism is making a more metaphysical claim. The problem is not simply the centrality or the exalted status that is often claimed for one's own self. It is the meaningfulness and the very existence of the self that is denied in Buddhism.[3] For many years, I have been attracted to process thought as a way of organizing my worldview. Many have noted the parallels between the process philosophy of such figures as Alfred North Whitehead and Charles Hartshorne and Buddhist views of the self. I feel more at home with process thought's view of existence as a series of inherited occasions. In process thought, a *dominant occasion* presides over my being, somewhat as self or mind or soul presides in other views, but the stress is on "occasion" rather than "dominant." The self is deeply in process. Continuity is provided by the inheritance of *earlier* occasions, as part of the definition of an *emerging* occasion. The emphasis, however, is on process. Process thought offers a Western version of a self in process.

And I have been interested in Derek Parfit's "branching self," in which each moment of new experience or decision causes the self to branch out from itself, then branch still more as life moves on. Parfit speaks of "ancestor selves" and "descendant selves," each finding its place on the branching tree. One can therefore speak of one's future selves or past selves. There is not a simple one-one relation between past selves and future selves, though there will be degrees of psychological connectedness. Parfit is interested in a number of important problems as he explores this view of personal identity, issues of responsibility, survival, and memory. The range of mind-body issues is linked to issues of identity. I share Parfit's interest in all these issues. But Parfit acknowledges that a belief in "the special nature of personal identity" can make people "more depressed by the thought of aging and of death."[4] I know that my own interest in this view is, to some degree, motivated by concern for issues of suffering and death.

3. Dunne, *All the Earth*, 51–56.
4. Parfit, "Personal Identity," 200.

There are significant differences between Buddhism, process thought, and Parfit's thought. They are all intellectually interesting. But I acknowledge that part of my interest comes from the thought that I don't need to be anxious about the future of myself if, in fact, my own self won't exist in the future. However, in the last analysis, I can't deny the self. This is not the place to argue for the endurance of the self, but others have done it.[5] My minor sense of guilt and my major sense of responsibility certainly contribute to an awareness of an enduring self. My own sense of the self feels more like a spiral staircase than like Parfit's branching tree. I circle around my own self through memory. I pick up events and experiences from the past, savoring and weighing and pondering them. They are transfigured each time I remember them, each time I weave them into the emerging self that gives the earlier fragments of my life new meaning. We move along in process, but we revisit the earlier self, holding it and building it into the emerging self.

For my present purposes, my conclusion is that I am *a significantly enduring self, a self who will actually die.*

Other views argue that the self doesn't become past, because nothing ever becomes past. This is the third denial on my index card musings from many months ago. One way of making this claim is to say that all things are held in God's eternity, which is beyond time with its various tenses. God holds past, present and future in one timeless Eternal Now. This kind of claim is standard for some forms of theism. Again, I am too deeply influenced by process thought to go very far with this.

The passage of time is real for God, just as it is real for us. The future is ontologically different from the past. Process thought speaks of God as "everlasting," rather than "eternal," in order to make this point. God is everlasting, inclusive of all time. But this "all time" doesn't blend into a homogenous Now. The past is past even for God; the future is future, even for God.

When we die, *we become significantly past.*

Of course, process theology has its own way of denying that our lives become past. A widely held view among process

5. Doepke, *Kinds of Things.*

theologians is the concept of "objective immortality." There is no subjective immortality of the self, but all events are held everlastingly in God's perfect memory. Life doesn't continue after death, but our lives are conserved exactly as they were in God's memory. The meaning and value of our lives becomes a part of God's ongoing life. The meaning of our lives is found in being able to enrich God's life (in that sense, to actually *create* the contingent aspect of God's being), as well as to have God suffer along with our sufferings.

I have spent much of my personal and professional life pondering "perpetual perishing." The way life is eroded by the passage of time, so that all experiences seem to be fleeting and transient, has occupied me more than the conclusion of our experiences by death. Many of my publications have explored the ways concern with perpetual perishing has manifested itself in our culture, particularly in art and literature.[6] The human need to believe in some conservation of the value of our lives shows up in diverse secular ways, as well as in religious settings.

For many years, the thought that my life contributed to and enriched God's life, and was everlastingly held in God's perfect memory, was a profound religious consolation for me. It was a far more subtle immortality than many versions in popular or sophisticated cultures, but it nourished me.

Over the years, I have begun to have serious doubts about the coherence of this view. There is no doubt that perpetual perishing is a profound human concern. I have begun to doubt, however, whether it is meaningful to speak of God's "memory," much less to claim that each occasion of our lives is held in that memory.

In an earlier, more technical article, I have explained in detail why I have these questions.[7] To say that God has a perfect memory is to use analogical language in speaking about God. Human memory offers an analogy by which we believe we can say that God has something like human memory, except that God's memory is "perfect." Even at the human level, however, the concept of

6. Dicken 2000, 2002a, 2004.
7. Dicken 2002b.

memory is highly metaphorical. Memory has been pictured as a room, an onion, a palimpsest, a computer, an archaeological layer, or a magic slate toy. What metaphor grounds the claim that God has "perfect" memory? I suspect that operative in such a claim is a metaphor somewhat like memory as a bank with constant, perfectly audited records.

A more basic problem with this analogy is that it now appears that human memory changes each time a particular memory is called up. The act of remembering seems to redefine the memory. Each act of summoning the memory adds an overlay to the memory. This seems to be true introspectively, experimentally, and in literary explorations of memory. Each time the madeleine summons a childhood memory for Marcel Proust, then that memory takes on a richer meaning.

If this is true, what would a "perfect" memory be? A perfect memory suggests a curiously non-process view of memory. A true process view of things would seem to suggest that memory itself is in process.

My skepticism of memory as offering an analogy for understanding God is part of a more general skepticism of the *via analogia*, the view that we can speak of God by borrowing analogies from human experience. I am drawn to the more odd ways of speaking of God: certainly parable, but also silence, paradox, gesture, and the various mystical ways of "unsaying."[8]

All of this leaves me unable to say that I believe God will remember either me or my life. It leaves me searching for a parable or a gesture or an unsaying that will articulate how I might nonetheless be held in God's grace.

There is a final denial that I can talk about more briefly. It would always be possible to dismiss the process of dying as not mattering because all of human life is meaningless. There can be an odd comfort in asserting the meaninglessness of human striving. If it doesn't mean anything, if nothing matters in the first place, then it doesn't matter that I am dying. Oddly enough, there could be a certain lightening of tone if nothing matters.

8. Sells, *Mystical Languages of Unsaying.*

It's not clear exactly which serious thinker affirms the mood I'm trying to describe. Certainly there are existentialist thinkers who teach the meaninglessness of things. But as I examine particular thinkers, the mood I'm describing doesn't quite fit. Albert Camus, for instance, can write about the absurdity of human living and dying. Yet there is also his affirmation of rebellion against the absurdity of life.

What I am describing is much more a widespread mood that is "around." Nothing matters in the long run and therefore it doesn't matter if I die. It will all be the same in the long run. It's not unlike a mood one occasionally encounters in post-modern writings. There are meanings, plenty of meanings. Everything has multiple meanings, all the meanings one could possibly want. But Meaning is suffocated by meanings. If meanings are all over the place, then there is no Meaning. As Mark Taylor puts it, ". . .the problem is not the lack of meaning but its excess."[9]

I want to deny the denial of meaning, in its existentialist, popular, or post-modern forms. I believe that fact and meaning cannot be separated, that we live in a world that we can only experience as saturated with meaning. With my four denials of the four denials, I see my situation (and everyone else's) as being that of *a meaningful self who will truly die and become really past.* I can't ease this situation by denying that I am a self, denying that I will really die, denying that I will become truly past, or denying that it even matters.

Of course, different combinations of these various denials and denials of denials are possible. It is possible to hold that there is an enduring self or soul that is immortal, which will be reunited with its body at a general resurrection, and will live in the presence of God in an Eternal Now. This is, in fact, a fairly orthodox Christian position.

I have not tried to argue in detail for my denials of the four denials. I have been more interested in outlining the range of issues and positions that interact with one another. I believe, however, that my position is held by a significant number of people, though

9. Taylor, *Hiding*, 56.

my way of outlining it may be new to them. In fact, based on my pastoral experience, I believe something like my view is held by a significant number of Christians for whom strict orthodoxy is not a primary concern. It is a position that may also be similar to that of many Jews.

As a young man in graduate school, I listened to H. Richard Niebuhr talk about "trusting the void." It was only after the death of the gods on which we relied, only after staring at the abyss, that we could begin to trust that void. To believe in God is to trust the void. "This reality, this nature of things, abides when all else passes. It is the source of all things and the end of all. It surrounds our life as the great abyss into which all things plunge and as the great source whence they all come. What it is we do not know save that it is and that it is the supreme reality with which we must reckon."[10]

It is one thing to memorize these words. It is another matter to be grounded only on an abyss. To speak of trusting the void is to engage in unsaying. Of course, to speak of "trusting" is to speak analogically, borrowing from the ordinary human experience of trusting. But to speak of "the void" is to move away from human analogy. It is a term that can have specific meaning in ordinary language, as when we might say that the President's address was void of any sense of personal accountability. But to use the term as Niebuhr uses it, as a way of imaging the whole of things, is to move towards unsaying. Yet such unsaying seems like highly accurate language to me.

John Dunne evokes a very similar vision in different language. John Dunne writes of the darkness before and after the light of our lives. Dunne writes, "Beyond this in either direction, past or future, is a time that is really not one's own, though one can in some manner bring this time also to mind. The problem is that time in the larger sense, the centuries, is no one's lifetime."[11] He calls this "the darkness that goes before life and comes after life."[12] For Dunne, God is found as we come to love, in the depths of our

10. Niebuhr, *Radical Monotheism*, 122.

11. Dunne, *The Search for God*, 170.

12. Ibid., 221.

souls, this darkness that encompasses our life stories. Loving the encompassing darkness is, it seems, very much like trusting the void.

I want to hold on to the light that my life seems to be. It is not easy to love the darkness. I remind myself of those aspects of the world that seem to be full of light, things such as consciousness of the world, interiority, memory, time, and the sense that some things are precious.

These aspects have emerged and they give us an increasingly complex sense of the world. As Niebuhr put it, we don't know what the ultimate is save that it is. Yet consciousness and consciousness of consciousness and self-consciousness or self-awareness are here. Memory, which no doubt originally served as an aid to survival, now is a mysterious realm in which we can wander, holding on to this and regretting that. Much of our life's meaning is merged with memory. With memory and its gift of a sustained past comes the awareness of time in all its tenses. And with this mixture emerges the ability to prefer one thing above another. Again, preference (or evaluating) is critical to survival, but it has become so much more. My academic side wants to say that value has emerged, but my real need is to say that the light in which we live now includes things that are *precious*, things that are to be *cherished*. Does my ability to ponder this richness make it easier for me to trust the void, to love the surrounding darkness?

There may be other complexities and greater richness of which I know nothing. If they emerged in a way I could comprehend, I might have more of a clue to the ultimate void, the encompassing darkness. But I can't conceive what they might be. Perhaps in some way, if I could see clearly, I would know both *that* and *how* my life and death have meaning. But I don't see clearly.

My friend Rem Edwards reminds me from time to time that the unexamined life is, as a matter of fact, worth living. To claim that only the examined life is worth living is philosophical snobbery, an idolatry of systemic intellectual values. Millions of people find life to be very much worth living, without engaging in the kind of careful examination that some of us find as natural as breathing.

I think there is a similar error involving theological imperialism. Simply because some of us, including myself, believe that there may be an overarching theological meaning to life *does not imply that we need to know what that meaning is* for our lives to have meaning. There may well be an ultimate meaning to life without our informed or knowing participation in that meaning being necessary. As I move towards a sense of a humanly incomprehensible God who may be spoken of only indirectly, it becomes necessary for me to observe these distinctions.

Does a humanly meaningful act need to have some other meaning for that original meaning to be stable? If it is worthwhile to sit talking late at night with a friend, does there need to be some other meaning—a theological meaning—for the intrinsic meaning to not dissolve before our very eyes as we examine it? Or, to shift the metaphor, is a theological meaning necessary to keep the intrinsic meaning from being eaten away by the cancer of meaninglessness? If there is a theological meaning that gives meaning to what already seems meaningful, is it necessary for us to *know* that theological meaning for it to be effective?

These are important questions for me as I die, because I am running out of time. I have spent my life searching for the meaning of life, exploring the various options as they branch out like one of Parfit's tree-selves. When I had a sense that there was plenty of time, much of the joy of life was tied up with the new order of books waiting to be read, the new recording to hear, the new friend to meet. The sense that there were more options to explore was part of the fun of things.

The joy of unending options has ended. I believe there is a mystery that is finally incomprehensible to human perceiving and conceiving. It can only be hinted at in indirect ways. It can only be said by not saying. The issue is whether I can trust this void, this emptiness. This trust in the void can only be actualized anew each time I live with joy without knowing what the meaning of my life is.

In an important article, Brooke Alan Trisel has examined a related problem. Does my life have any meaning if the human race becomes extinct at some point in the future? This is perhaps a secular version of the problem some of us pick at in more theological terms. Trisel points out that it is writers and artists who tend to define their life's meaning in terms of influence on later generations. He mentions people who deliver the mail and those who care for others in a hospital as examples of people who might have a very different view. Their impact is immediate. They might not have nearly the intense interest in their long-range influence.

Trisel builds a convincing case for the thought that an act or event either has immediate meaning or it doesn't. To have long-range impact determine its meaning seems odd. If it was known that all human life would end in two weeks, we would think it odd if a man chose not to pull his daughter from a well, where she was in great pain, because it wouldn't make any difference in two weeks anyway.[13]

It certainly makes sense to attach value to actions that will only be completed after one's death, such as work on a cure for cancer or trying to be a good parent. But this is different from having the meaning of our lives depend on an infinite extension of human meaning.

I think a similar point can be made about the need for an overarching theological meaning. Do we need some *Meaning* to give meaning to aspects of our lives that already *seem* meaningful? If so, does that *Meaning* itself need some *Super-Meaning* to give meaning to it?

I have trouble conceiving what kind of theological Meaning can give meaning to my life. I don't think some form of personal immortality would do the job, if we haven't first of all solved the problem of perpetual perishing. What good could it do me to go on forever if all the meaning in my life doesn't accumulate, but rather gets eroded by time, slipping away into the past? I doubt that I can remember one percent of the days I have lived. Why keep at it forever?

13. Trisel, *Human Extinction*, 387.

If, on the other hand, we respond to perpetual perishing with the idea of God's perfect memory, I cannot conceive what we end up with that might give meaning to me as I sit here, typing and dying, as you sit there reading and dying. If I try to picture a final state of God's memory, it might include me, but I'm not clear how that is a meaning for me, rather than a meaning for God. If I dismiss the idea of a final state of God's memory, and conceive the memory instead as adding to an everlastingly ongoing story, an interesting narrative might evolve, but it's God's narrative, not mine. The essence of monotheism, I believe, is the conviction that God is more important than I am. But I still need to ask about the meaning of my life in light of that reality. How does God's Meaning give meaning to my meaning?

I'm not claiming that there is no ultimate meaning. I'm only claiming that whatever meaning there may be is inconceivable and unsayable by me. This "what it is we do not know save that it is" (in Niebuhr's terms) may well have its own agenda in which my life makes perfect sense. But terms such as "meaning" or "purpose of life" are my own highly conditioned terms. I can't say what relation such terms may have to the void, the darkness that encompasses my life.

The fact is I would rather live my life as I am now living it for two years rather than one year, for five years rather than two years. At any given moment I would prefer to embrace my wife, to search for the right word, to stare off into space, than not to do so. I don't know what difference it makes, but I would rather live.

14 GOD FOR AN OLD MAN

I

As I finish the eighth decade of my life, it is time to confront the issue of what really matters to me, of how I really understand things. My purpose here is not to display critical skills, writing about the great thinkers who have influenced me. My concern here is to say in rather simple language how I want to sum up things. I remember reading years ago Somerset Maugham's memoir *The Summing Up*. I may not get to a sum, but I can perhaps get through an equation or two.

I am interested in what lingers in my life from the past: memories of loved ones, snatches of music from the 1950s, hurts that I don't want to talk about, catching fireflies and putting them in a jar, puberty, and the wonderful discovery that there exist other people who also like to think about things.

It is not only personal memories that linger. The Civil War, for instance, lingers anywhere you drive in the eastern United States, both in place names and in present day issues. When my wife and I drive into Louisville for a day, we drive through a patch of exposed rock 60 feet high on either side. When the Interstate system was being built, Interstate 64 (as well as many other similar patches of road) cut through many geological layers. Those exposed layers are all over the United States. We drive through a patch of space and, at the same time, we go back in time, wondering as we drive about the many stories that are suggested by that rock. I learned from John McPhee's books on geology that these exposed rocks provide a great opportunity for geologists. McPhee tells stories of driving with geologists and pulling over, hiking back to the exposed layers as cars whizzed by, and watching and listening as the geologist pokes around, describing to McPhee events from millions of years ago.[1] The past lingers in strange places.

There are things that linger, but there are also things that lure. I am lured by many kinds of things: tonight's dinner, a planned trip, a visit from a grandchild, a new book. But some lures move well beyond that. I long for world peace. I want all children to have enough to eat. I learned to use the word "lure" while reading the philosopher Alfred North Whitehead. Whitehead said that we are lured by "eternal objects," possibilities that are offered to us in each moment or occasion of life. I don't know about that, but I do know that lures are part of my humanity. Whitehead also knew about things that linger, though he did not use my word "linger."[2] I have wondered whether perhaps a child is more defined by lures, while older people have more lingering thoughts. Certainly a normal lifespan suggests that a child has a longer future, while the grandparent has a longer past. However, I don't think that is the issue. Children have been busy. As one example, they have been learning a foreign language (their native language), a language that lingers in and defines their minds. A language involves lots of words, rules, and colloquialisms to remember. I think older people are deeply lured, though perhaps we talk more than we should about the past. It bothers us that important things (people, events, struggles) are missed by younger people because they were born too late. At times, it is hard not to remind them of what they missed.

These times of pondering things that both linger and lure can stretch out for a while. I can move effortlessly between what lingers and what lures as they blend into one another and pull me

1. McPhee, *The Former World*, 21–24, 210.
2. Whitehead, *Process and Reality*, 346–351.

towards themselves. It is in those times that I am truly present to my past, present to my future, present to my presence. I am there in the present and usually realize with a jolt that I have been "lost in thought," though I am actually not lost at all.

It has occurred to me that my inclusive sense of all that *lingers* in my mood of presence does some of the work of traditional doctrines of creation. I am created by all that lingers. And my sense of all that *lures* in that same mood or mode of presence is my version of eschatology. Maybe God is the sort of thing you have to chisel out for yourself, over the years, if doing that kind of thing interests a person. My chiseled God is simpler than some versions. It is more like modern sculpture, perhaps suggestive of a Henry Moore sculpture, rather than a detailed, realistic picture of God. A realistic image of God would be unrealistic because we can't be precise about these issues. When telling of my God, I am also telling of myself. When that which lingers and that which lures come together, and we are immersed in one of those moments of presence between past and future, that present moment can actually last for a while. It is then that I am present to my own presence. It is then that the mystery of life gives me the freedom to be present.

II

Sometimes writers of fiction can get at things in deep ways that those of us who lean towards philosophy and theology can't quite say. I am interested in the idea of presence, what I might call "deep presence." Presence, as I use the term, is not a thing, but it is a reality.

> A baby is born; his mother holds him. She looks at the lush pink of his lips, luxuriant as if they were already sated from a lifetime of pleasures. His fingers close around one of his mother's fingers. His toenails glisten like specks of abalone. His ears are as marvelously convoluted as any Escher drawing, the lobes are tiny teardrops. His mother

examines his ears, knowing they are portals to the part of him that is not there. The baby is anencephalic. There is no brain. He will die in 57 hours, while his mother holds him.

The first four pages of Leah Hager Cohen's novel *The Grief of Others* lay out this scene. My language describing the baby is borrowed from Cohen's writing, though I have not cluttered it with short specific quotes. After this four-page setting, the rest of the novel explores the impact of this event on others, as the baby's family and others strive to deal with one another and this central fact.[3]

As Susann Cokal describes Cohen's writing in her review of the book, "She drives home our ability, even our need, to love without reason, to attach to something small and doomed simply because it exists."[4]

In her novel *No Book but the World*, Cohen writes of a young woman and her younger brother. The brother seemed always to find life difficult, shunning most human contact, preferring to be by himself in the small woods near their home, avoiding the disciplines imposed by school and other people, happiest when he was by himself, with no place but the world. After they are both grown, the body of a young boy is found in those same woods and suspicion, of course, begins to focus on her brother. The sister returns home to look in on her brother in jail and to visit his lawyer.

Cohen describes a scene in which the sister decides to attend the community service of mourning after the death of the young boy. Her younger brother, who has long struggled trying to cope with life, is suspected of having some culpability in the death. The service concludes with an older woman singing "Old Joe Clark," the favorite song of the dead boy. As she sings slowly, deliberately, beautifully, and mournfully, the sister, who didn't even know the dead boy, ponders.

3. Cohen, *Grief of Others*, 3–6.
4. Cokal, *Review*, 10.

One feels he must be here unseen, listening, drinking in her voice that is for him and him alone. I get the queerest feeling that we are the ghosts, shadowy, insubstantial, congregated here only to witness the living communion that is occurring between this old woman, this newly dead child, of an old woman who sings of Old Joe Clark as if she was singing only to the dead boy, while others listen to her as she does that.[5]

Cohen is a wonderful writer who can say that the mourners were "drinking in her voice," a mixed metaphor that the reader understands is exactly the right metaphor. This is how humans experience life. The boy is not present, just as the baby whose brain has not developed is not present. Yet I find myself moved by the sense that they are each, indeed, in some way, present. We can understand such moments. We think of and we talk to people who are not there. The dead boy is present to the old woman just as she, in turn, is present to those listening.

I add one more quote from an earlier writer, Flannery O'Connor. In her inimitable way, O'Connor describes conflicting insights in her description of what she calls "the idiot child" Bishop. Bishop's uncle and guardian Rayber can look at the child as a sign of "the general hideousness of fate." But at certain moments he can be overwhelmed by a love for Bishop.

Anything he looked at too long could bring it on. Bishop did not have to be around. It could be a stick or a stone, the line of a shadow, the absurd old man's walk of a starling crossing the sidewalk. If, without thinking, he lent himself to it, he would feel suddenly a morbid surge of the love that terrified him powerful enough to throw him to the ground in an act of idiot praise. It was completely irrational and abnormal. . . .

It was love without reason, love for something futureless, love that appeared to exist only to be itself, imperious and all demanding, the kind that would cause him to make a fool of himself in an instant.[6]

5. Cohen, *No Book*, 148–149.

6. O'Connor, *Three*, 372.

It is inevitable in O'Connor's stark vision, though nonetheless still shocking, that Bishop will eventually be both drowned and baptized in the same action, since baptism is itself a description of a provocative insight into dying and life. Baptism is an act of drowning, of letting the old life die, in order to be open to a new life.

I quote these writers of fiction to suggest that human life itself seems to dial up or intensify the importance of presence. The wording with which we can describe presence is not precise, but the presence of presence is, at times, crucial in human life. This is the case among humans. This means that humans find themselves cherishing realities that seem to have no practical or utilitarian value. Our everyday value system does not fully account for those moments that become precious to us. These are often moments of a sense of something present that we have trouble defining, moments that could be seen as useless, though they are definitive for a human way of being.

III

This way of being, pondering both that which lingers and also all that lures me, often happens in a room I use as a study. It has no phone, no computer, no television. It has shelves of books and comfortable chairs. I have some of my favorite art on the walls. The art ranges from drawings made for me by grandchildren to reproductions of work by Mark Rothko (No. 6, Violet, Green and Red, 1951), Rene Magritte, and others, works that both linger and lure.

Most importantly, large windows surround me, so that I can watch the sky, trees, rabbits, squirrels, woodchucks, stray cats, and many birds. It is here that I can most naturally pause between what lingers and what lures. This is a time when I can be present to my own presence, aware that I am, at that moment, a presence to myself. When I "come to myself," whatever that may mean, I often have been lingering in that state of affairs for ten or fifteen minutes, even for an hour on a few occasions.

In such extended moments, I can begin to think of all that surrounds me. We spend much of our lives trying to seek out and understand what surrounds us. As a child, I tried to figure out my parents and older sister, then my schoolmates, then the larger world through which I was learning to move. Sitting in my study, I think about all the changes that have taken place in that larger world during my life and the changes in my ways of trying to understand.

And I go beyond the world (in the sense of our earth). I must have been about eight years old when an uncle who was visiting us came out on our front porch and joined me on a swing. "Look at that sky," he said. "Look at those stars." He told me that he sometimes spent hours looking at the sky on a clear night. He said that he wondered about those stars. He told me they were millions of miles away.

Of course, the night sky was much more visible in the 1940s than it is now. But I still think of my uncle and his comments when I remember to look at the sky. The sky is much more complex than he could have imagined. Even though most of us are not astronomers, many of us read works by those who are skilled at writing in an accessible way about complex scientific work. We have become accustomed to hearing talk of black holes, galaxies, the expanding universe, the big bang, entropy, gravity and mysterious forces. And we stare at the beauty of the night sky with wonder and awe. And we wonder what it all means.

For many of us, these difficult-to-define issues raise the question of God. For a long time, many people have thought of God as that which is all-encompassing, enclosing all that exists in God's own being. J.B. Philips' *Your God is Too Small* influenced people in the twentieth century to envision a God great enough to encompass the universe.

Of course, Alfred North Whitehead made a major contribution to the idea of panentheism, an all-inclusive God. Everything in the world is in process and God also is in process. God is the all-inclusive event that lures the finite events of the world, is enriched by them, suffers with them, and holds them in the divine memory. Whitehead's vocabulary can be notoriously difficult, but the essence of his work is accessible to many people. Whitehead's God is one who experiences us experiencing the world.[7]

It is a rich understanding of God, developed in great detail by Charles Hartshorne and many other process thinkers. For some of these thinkers, the existence of God is assured by the ontological argument. Indeed, Hartshorne liked to point out that the development of process thought enriched and clarified the idea of God so that we now know that it is an all-inclusive God, enriched in an ongoing way by the world, that offers a clear definition of a "greatest conceivable being."[8] That greatest conceivable being is growing in its greatness as it is enriched by an evolving world.

This seems to imply that some kind of world is itself necessary to God, the greatest conceivable being. God's contingent nature, inclusive of the universe, is great because of that inclusiveness.

Of course, many scientists, as well as many non-scientists, would claim that we have no way of knowing that there is a God over and beyond whatever is included in the universe. Just as it is not clear what we might mean by "God," it is not even clear what might be meant by "universe."

Is "universe" a reality of some kind? Or is it simply a useful term for the great sum total of all things? And, of course, some have held that we should also think about multiverses, many universes, each of them more or less complete in itself.[9] Is the universe the container of all things? Or is it God's awareness of everything that makes it a universe?

We learn that the Second Law of Thermodynamics tells us that, even though energy is neither created nor destroyed, it becomes randomly distributed and therefore unavailable for doing anything of interest to us, even such things as helping us think about these things.

Which is it? There is either a universe subject to increasing entropy or an increasingly enriched and enriching God. That

7. Whitehead, *Process and Reality.*

8. Hartshorne, *Anselm's Discovery*, 3–21.

9. Rubenstein 2014.

seems to be one thing we might ponder as we try to understand what it means to believe in God.

These are the sorts of things I think about when I ponder what surrounds me and encompasses me.

I often wonder how the story of Jesus relates to these cosmic concerns. I learned the story of Jesus as a child. As an adult, I became interested in "the search for the historical Jesus" and read most of the studies in that field. I am interested in some of the other early accounts that also are being discovered, such as some Gnostic gospels, but those versions of Jesus were not what originally shaped me. I am less interested in getting those issues resolved than I am in the story about Jesus that has come down to us, an amalgam of the four biblical Gospels. It is the received story of Jesus that lingers in my life, rather than the "historical" Jesus. I am more interested in the *transformative* story of Jesus than in the "real" history.[10] I pick and choose what I like from that story, for my own personal needs and commitments, though so does everyone else.

My concern here is with the tension between the story of Jesus (and its foundational story of the law and the prophets that came before him) and what is sometimes called deep space and deep time. How can a couple of years of a man's life, lived in a few square miles, be related to cosmic eons? To millions of galaxies? To cosmic black holes? It is not easy to define this issue carefully, but the two versions of reality don't seem to fit together neatly like a jigsaw puzzle. Though few of us are cosmic physicists or astronomers, there are well-written, readable accounts of emerging science by good writers, such as Neil LeGrasse Tyson.[11] Many people today have a wide background sense influenced by science. This is really a more important issue than the evolution of life forms, an issue that often gets more publicity.

The attempt to find some signals or indications of intelligent life in other parts of the universe seems to be motivated in part by a background sense of cosmic loneliness. It is as if the more

10. Dicken, "Biblical Picture of Jesus."

11. Tyson, *Death By Black Holes.*

pervasive existence of intelligence in the universe would somehow make our own existence more understandable, perhaps more "fitting" into things.

The point is sometimes made that, unfathomable as our universe might be, humans are the ones who have probed and discovered the reality of all that. Though we may be daunted by the awesome images of astronomy, nonetheless, it is the brains of astronomers, their searching minds, which give us this understanding. Humans are astronomers; God is, somehow, a mathematician.

It is obvious that the human mind, and its ways of thinking, pose the issue of human meaning in our universe. That mind is also a *clue* that needs to be taken seriously in our reflections.

The great scientist Freeman Dyson writes in an accessible way about many of these issues. I have appreciated a comment in his Gifford Lectures.

> Like the majority of scientists in this century, I have not concerned myself seriously with theology. Theology is a foreign language which we have not taken the trouble to learn. My personal theology is the theology of an amateur. But I once did have some help from a professional theologian in formulating my ideas in an intellectually coherent fashion. I happened to meet Charles Hartshorne at a meeting in Minnesota and we had a serious conversation. After we had talked for a while he informed me that my theological standpoint is Socinian. Socinus was an Italian heretic who lived in the sixteenth century. If I remember correctly what Hartshorne said, the main tenet of the Socinian heresy is that God is neither omniscient nor omnipotent. He learns and grows as the universe unfolds. I do not pretend to understand the theological subtleties to which this doctrine leads if one analyzes it in detail. I merely find it congenial, and consistent with common sense. I do not make any clear distinction between mind and God. God is what mind becomes when it has passed beyond the scale of our comprehension.[12]

12. Dyson, *Infinite*, 119.

I have never had the opportunity to meet either Hartshorne or Dyson, but as I read this paragraph, I feel as if I am eavesdropping on two old friends. Process thinkers might quibble about the meaning of omniscience, since a process view holds that God's increasing knowledge as the world unfolds is, in fact, omniscience. My concern here is to suggest an even more rich understanding of mind. It is appropriate to think of the minds of mathematicians and astronomers as factors to be remembered when we ponder a modern version of the cosmos. However, there are other depths of human minds that should not be forgotten. The minds of artists and musicians also tell us something about human nature and its place in the great expanses of nature. There is also the reality of morality as an aspect of human life, even if we often have trouble living up to our own moral codes.

It is against this backdrop that I would point out that Jesus gives us a story of a human in this same cosmos. He is not famous as an astronomer, though he noted the colors of the sky. He fills out our understanding of what it can mean to be a human. He is remembered as one who embodied other aspects of the self than mathematics or art. He embodied a love that is more than simply a moral code. He was angry with other humans who diminished or judged their fellow humans too quickly or too superficially. He embodied forgiveness. He emphasized the love of the poor and the hungry. His very presence seemed to heal people. He lived in the constant presence of his Abba God, except for the one time on the cross when he was stunned by the absence of God. Surely all this is part of what can be meant by a human life in an immense cosmos.

How that all comes together is an issue for me as I try to put things together, sitting in my study. The story of Jesus offers us an aspect of human selfhood or mind that also needs to be considered, if we are going to interpret the universe in terms of the presence of minds that can penetrate deeply into mathematics and astronomy.

Whitehead tells us that God encompasses us, contains us, envelopes us, knows it all as it all unfolds. God, he wrote, lures the world like a poet, trying to complete or at least continue the cosmic poem.[13] Perhaps, I might modestly suggest, just a bit like an old man sitting in his study, one who is present to his own presence.

IV

I search that which lingers from the past and that which lures from the future. I explore all that surrounds us and I try to make some personal sense of the universe and an all-encompassing God.

There is one more direction I want to take as I write about these things. As I explore my own life, and seek to probe my awareness of God, I often find myself moving inward. Our most deeply personal direction takes place when we make that move inward. The word "inward" is clearly a metaphor, since I am still sitting in the same chair, looking out the same windows. I move inward, I probe more deeply, my concern is with my self. That previous sentence is saturated with metaphor. Nonetheless, it is one direction we can go to seek ourselves and to seek God.

Paul Tillich wrote of "the dimension of depth." This is not a dimension that we can measure with a yardstick or a compass. Yet his language spoke deeply to a generation of Americans in the mid-twentieth century.

As I probe my own inner being, I know there is anger down there. I have worked much of my life trying to make sure that I am angry about the right things. There are hurts. There is guilt for wounds I have inflicted. There is a level of self that I can only call a deep level, a level of depth, where things hide from me, and I hide from them. There is anxiety over the very death I have, for the most part, made my peace with. There is fear of pain as I grow older. There is a fear of falling.

At this stage of life, a person begins to lose some things. Loved ones and friends have died. It is not as easy to move around. But the great fear is of losing oneself, losing one's mind. The ability to remember, to ponder and sort through things, is definitive for

---

13. Whitehead, *Process and Reality*, 346.

human life. Older people fear losing the ground of selfhood, of losing all that lingers.

Most of all, there is a fear of losing my memory, my own presence to myself. St. Augustine could not go very far in his *Confessions* without devoting a couple of searching chapters to the subject of memory.[14] If we had no memory, we would not be fully human. Augustine saw that memory is also a link to God. But as we age in today's world, we watch carefully to see if we can detect a loss of memory and are terrified by the very thought of Alzheimer's Disease, more afraid even than we are of cancer or heart disease. We feel we can tough out most diseases, but we can't even imagine what it might be like to tough out Alzheimer's Syndrome. It seems it would be the loss of our very life and of our very God. If we had no memory, we could not be aware of the presence of God. God might be present, but we could not relate that to our lives or to our environs.

As Karsten Harries puts it, writing of St. Augustine, "Memory attests to the spirit's power to transcend time, just as the imagination attests to its power to transcend space."[15]

A few decades ago, immersed in Paul Tillich's thought, I was impressed with his comment that to "exist" literally means to "stand out." A few moments with the Oxford English Dictionary convinced me that he was right. In his own distinctive way, Tillich wrote that what an existing thing stands out from is non-being.

Over the years, I have pondered that sense of existence and noticed the ways language assumes such a view. It is not very difficult to sense our own existences as standing out from nothingness. We brood over death and we experience ourselves as moving through the midst of many other existences, other things that themselves stand out from still other things that also stand out.

Paul Tillich spoke of God as the ground of being, the ultimate foundation that enables all the specific convex beings to "stand out" from non-being. "Ground" has a reassuring quality to it. Whether

14. There are many available versions of Augustine's *Confessions*. It is in Sections X and XI that Augustine discusses memory.

15. Harries, *Infinity and Perspective*, 155.

we think of the ground as the premise of a logical argument, the basis from which we can reason, or simply as the support underneath us, the earth upon which we stand, or perhaps even as an electrical grounding, there is a deep security in being grounded.

Tillich's most interesting exploration is in his Terry Lectures *The Courage to Be*. He explores three major anxieties of human life: death, guilt, and meaninglessness. For Tillich, anxiety about meaninglessness is a distinctively modern anxiety. In the face of each of these threats, humans need to find "the courage to be." We need to find a courage that is grounded beyond any *existing* reality, anything that might merely "stand out" with the same vulnerability that we share. The courage that allows us *to be* in the very depths of our being is God, the ground of our being. This ground is the ultimate support of all things. It is not a being among others. It is the ground of being. The ground of being does not exist or stand out; existing things stand out from the ground. God, conceived in this way, is not a particular being, but rather (perhaps worthy of capitalization) "Being Itself."

It continues to be startling for people who learn that many thoughtful believers in God do not think that God exists. God doesn't stand out from being; God is Being Itself. From this non-existing power of being we draw our own existences, our own courage to be in the face of death, guilt, and meaninglessness.

V

The very idea of God began to emerge only a few thousand years ago, though humans have been around a few hundred thousand or so years. Certainly, any *writing* about God is very recent. These writings are based on earlier stories, shared by word of mouth for some years before being written down. People speak as if the idea of God has been around for a long time. It hasn't. Anthropologists suggest that humans began with sacred spaces and sacred times, with the idea of a specific God emerging from that context.[16]

16. Bellah 2011.

Roman Catholic theologian John Dunne suggested that once upon a time God was here, now God is not here, and someday God will be here again.[17] In our secularized world today, there seems to be less focus on a living God. I am speaking here of God as something in human awareness. In this sense, I am writing at a very early stage of human thought about or experience of God. Our awareness of God will shift over the eons of the future. Perhaps some other word will emerge that better serves the purpose of addressing these issues.

There is that which *lingers*, that which *lures* us, that which *surrounds* us, as well as that which *grounds* us in our deepest, most inward being. These four patterns or dimensions are four of the major ways that we can evoke an awareness of or an understanding of God, a God who lingers from our past, lures from our future, surrounds us and grounds us. Time and space, as we experience them (in today's science-influenced world), are the triggers for these kinds of experience.

Coming to faith in God (or losing faith in God) seems to be very much like gaining an insight or having a new, different insight. Much of our progress will be along the lines of insights that emerge. One comes to faith in God or loses God through insights.

It is my purpose in this section to explore the nature of insight and its importance as humans seek to plumb the deepest issues they can ever confront. Insight is similar in some ways to its verbal neighbor "sight." It is possible to visually see things in two ways. It is like seeing the cliff dwellings of Mesa Verde from a distance. On December 18, 1888, Richard Wetherill and Charlie Mason, two cowboys from Mancos, found what is now called Cliff Palace in Mesa Verde after spotting the ruins from the top of the mesa. Wetherill gave the ruin its present-day name. He had heard native Americans say that their ancestors had dwelled in the cliffs, but white settlers could not figure out where it might have been. Today, one can stand very near to Wetherill's original spot. The dwellings are not there, then they are, and then a moment later the dwellings seem to disappear again, leaving only a ragged rock wall.

17. Dunne, *A Search for God*, 169–205.

At a deeper level, it is possible to conceive or imagine or understand things in two different ways. This is the level of insight, rather than sight. I focus on human awareness of God and the human dismissal of God as final, ultimate, inclusive ways of understanding things.

Too often, we discuss God in terms of faith or lack of faith (or even in terms of proof or disproof). I suggest it is better to examine issues in terms of insights that lead towards God or away from God. For years, I have been interested in personal accounts that people have given, as they have described how they came to hold certain perspectives on the major issues of life. In this section, I describe the ways the Catholic monk Thomas Merton, the members of the Shiloh religious community, and Dalia Eshkenazi came to their various insights. These are meant to be suggestive of the patterns that take shape in the lives of many others.

I have stood at the corner of Fourth and Walnut streets in Louisville many times since the 1940s. It's a central spot in downtown Louisville. In the 1940s, I stared at the young men in uniform, on Saturday leave from nearby Fort Knox. They traveled in small packs of three or four. I thought about how much fun it must be to be a soldier in World War II. Back then, civilian men dressed in suits to go downtown for shopping. At that age, I did not notice how women dressed.

Over the years, that corner has changed. Walnut Street is now Muhammad Ali Boulevard, named after a much beloved (at long last) native of Louisville. A plaque has been installed at the corner, describing Thomas Merton's experience at that spot. Merton, a Cistercian monk at nearby Gethsemani Monastery, was well-known as the author of *The Seven Storey Mountain*, a memoir of his days as a young man in the intellectual circles of New York City, his conversion to Catholicism, and his decision to enter the monastic life. He wrote profound studies of the devotional life, wrote against American involvement in the Vietnam War, and began to ponder the relationship of Christianity to Buddhism during his last years.

One day (March 19, 1958) he stood at the corner of Fourth and Walnut and watched the busy crowd of people around him.

This was back in the days when downtown was the place to see and be seen. Merton had an insight into the mob of humanity. He loved the people, the ordinary, real people who moved around him. The experience was powerful enough that he wrote about it that day in his diary, then later in a published work.[18] It is that almost mystical insight that the plaque commemorates.

Today, I still watch people on Fourth Street. I have had many thoughts about those people over the years. I think about those Fort Knox soldiers in a much different way now than I did as a small child. I would use a word such as "interesting" to describe my reactions to all those people over the years. A few times, in the 1980s, I felt vaguely threatened and walked along at a faster pace. However, I have never had a unified, overwhelming discovery of love for the human race, a sense that I was really one of that great gathering of people. Rather, I have more often experienced my inner privacy, distinguishing myself from all those others.

I have worked with the same data that Thomas Merton had before him, but any insights I have had have differed from his. That is the nature of insight. The same data is there before you, but it is seen in differing ways.

Insight can be determinative for religious views, determinative in both directions. Shirley Nelson gives a compelling account of Shiloh, a fundamentalist and apocalyptic religious community built on a hill in Maine during the early 1900s by Frank Sanford, an apparently charismatic leader. The community involving hundreds of people at its peak was molded by Sanford's insightful and yet damaged personality. There was often widespread hunger and illness among the devout people who followed Sanford, who always seemed to have plenty to eat and money to spend. Nelson tells the story with sensitivity, herself a descendent of parents and grandparents who were faithful members.

Nelson writes of a key moment in the life of her father Arnold, who grew up in the community. "Then, as if it had suddenly been shaken loose in his brain, an idea slid down that chain of thought and fell into his hands. There was no God. It was as simple

18. Merton, *Conjectures.*

as that. He had never actually believed that there was one, or not one that cared a shred about his own existence. For just an instant he stared at this, a recognition so bright he thought it would blind him. Then he dropped it."[19] After some hesitant months, Arnold left the community and was a rather outspoken atheist the rest of his life. His wife, who also grew up in the community, retained a more ambiguous stance, recognizing the faults in Sanford's leadership, yet holding a deeper loyalty to much that the community had stood for. Their daughter, Shirley Nelson, tells the story of all those good people with delicate understanding.

Sanford himself served several years in a federal prison in Georgia, for abusive and negligent leadership, demonstrated particularly during a missionary trip aboard his yacht and the group's schooner. Several people died as a result of his "faith" inspired decisions. Yet he moved to a position of leadership even among his fellow prisoners.

> Years earlier he had instituted at Shiloh what some called 'closed communion,'—that is, the ceremony could be shared only by those in full fellowship with Shiloh's creed and principles. In the prison, communion served by the chaplain, was 'open' indeed, shared not only by persons of mixed religious beliefs, but with murderers and thieves and rapists. For this reason Sanford had never gone to communion in prison. Then one Sunday in 1917 he saw the matter in a new light. In that mixed group were many of his own Bible class students, who might be confused by his detachment. As he filed out of Sunday service with the other prisoners, God said 'Turn,' and he entered the room designated for communion. It was the first ecumenical gesture he had made in almost twenty-five years.[20]

A profound insight can be disturbing and lead to differing ways of looking at things, differing ways of noticing, valuing, or discerning things.

---

19. Nelson, *Fair, Clear, and Terrible*, 375.

20. Ibid., 379–380.

Dalia Eshkenazi was one of the Jews whose families were able to buy a home from the government after Palestinians had been forced to flee those homes in the war of 1967. Sandy Tolan's book *The Lemon Tree* tells her story and the story of Bashir Khari, whose Palestinian family had fled that particular home. It is a moving account of two people struggling to know and understand one another years later. Against this very personal backdrop, Tolan is able to explore the larger story and its issues.

One comment in the book stands out. Dalia had grown up as a secular Jew, though her own belief in God had always been part of her. A good deal of that aspect of her which believed in God was infused with anger, as she learned about the Holocaust. For God to have allowed that to happen, she would recall thinking at the time, was "utterly unconscionable." Her anger included Christians who had been silent during those years. By the age of nine, she took piano lessons at a Catholic monastery. As she experienced the monastery's silence, a statue of St. Joseph, a portrait of Pope John XXIII's humane face, and the dimly lit corridors, a different presence began to engulf her. "Decades later, she would remember this moment as the beginning of a life of discernment: of being able to see the whole and not judge someone or something based simply on a single observation or teaching."[21] Tolan's book is an account of Dalia's attempt to be a discerning person in her very specific setting and history, particularly in her relationship with Bashir Khari.

Discernment, according to the Oxford English Dictionary, is to see things as distinct, to distinguish, to recognize a difference or to make a distinction. Tolan emphasizes Dalia's ability to see the whole as those distinctions get made.

In these three accounts, we see the way critical insights took place and shaped human lives.

One aspect of believing in God is to live a life of discernment. It is to see things in light of the whole and to notice particular things in that whole. It is a life of noticing and valuing in a certain way. To believe in God is, among other things, to notice certain things and interpret and value them in distinctive ways.

21. Tolan, *Lemon Tree*, 115.

Mary-Jane Rubenstein has a wonderful book tracing carefully the complex history of the concepts of wonder and awe. Wonder is the awareness that, according to Socrates/Plato, is the source of all philosophy. Awe is the awareness expressed by J. Robert Oppenheimer in his famous exclamation on viewing the first atomic explosion. Both wonder and awe continue as widely available ways of being in today's world. They seem to be aspects of the human experience of God, yet atheists also claim, very rightly, that wonder and awe are quite available to them as ways of contemplating the universe as people understand it today.

Mary-Jane Rubenstein writes of our human sense of "wonder." She details carefully the roots of that theme in early Platonic writing and traces it up through such thinkers as Jacques Derrida. Her most insightful writing, however, is in her own conclusion of the book. She suggests that wonder is not simply an abstract idea. It is literally something we live, something we inhale. The way we breathe affects our sense of wonder; wonder affects the way we breathe.

> Terror and amazement, horror and admiration, anger and resolution, repulsion and fascination, distress and expectation, taking in and letting go. The wonderer wonders: jaw dropped in astonishment, incomprehension, anticipation, rage; ears trained on what calls for help, for justice, for thought; eyes wide open to the absence of sense, the limits of knowledge, the touch of all things that opens out possibility. Perhaps that is it, then: perhaps dwelling in wonder is merely a matter of learning to breathe.[22]

Every other intense emotion or awareness is experienced in the ways we inhale. There is no obvious reason why the awareness of God should be any different. Many spiritual exercises, both religious and secular, are tied up with learning how to breathe.

I sit in my room surrounded by books, art, and windows open to the world. I watch the seasons change in front of me. I think of all these things. Sometimes I have my arms spread widely,

22. Rubenstein, *Strange Wonder*, 195–196.

my eyes open to whatever visits me, the way some people pray, ready to receive what comes. Sometimes I have my hands folded, my head bowed, my body turned in towards itself, the way some other people pray. I watch the way I breathe and try to be open to whatever comes to lure me. I always say a few words of prayer for world peace and for the poor. I usually pray a simple prayer for a few people by name. I am present there. I wait for whatever comes.

BIBLIOGRAPHY

Augustine, *Confessions*. Trans. Henry Chadwick. Oxford: Oxford University Press, 2008.

Bellah, Robert N. *Religion in Human Evolution: From the Paleolithic to the Axial Age*. Cambridge, Mass: Harvard University Press, 2011.

Becker, Ernest. *The Denial of Death*. New York: Peter Smith, 1998.

Bonhoeffer, Dietrich. *Letters and Papers From Prison*. London: SCM Press, 1967.

Borges, Jorge Luis. "Pascal's Sphere" in *Selected Non-Fictions*. New York: Viking, 1999.

Brock, Rita Nakashima and Rebecca Ann Parker. *Proverbs of Ashes*. Boston: Beacon, 2001.

Caputo, John D. *The Weakness of God: A Theology of the Event*. Bloomington, IN: Indiana University Press, 2006.

Rita Charon, *Narrative Medicine: Honoring the Stories of Illness*. New York: Oxford University Press, 2006.

Cohen, Leah Hager. *The Grief of Others*. New York: Riverhead Books, 2011.

———. *No Book but the World*. New York: Riverhead, 2014.

Cokal, Susan. Review of Leah Hager Cohen, *The Grief of Others*. The New York Times Book Review, September 18, 2011, p. 10.

Derrida, Jacques. *Memoirs of the Blind: The Self-Portrait and Other Ruins*. Chicago: University of Chicago Press, 2007.

Dicken, Thomas M. "Against Perishing: Reflections on Time and the Conservation of Value in Twentieth-Century Literature." *Soundings: An Interdisciplinary Journal*, 83:2 (2000), 361–383.

———. "The Biblical Picture of Jesus as the Christ in Tillich's Theology." *Journal of Religious Thought*, 25:1 (1968–1969), pp. 27–41.

———. "Charles Hartshorne on the Conservation of Value." *Process Studies*, 31.2 (Fall/Winter 2002), 32–50.

———. "Dying: An Interim Report." *Soundings: An Interdisciplinary Journal*, XC 3–4 (Fall/Winter 2007), 285–297.

———. "God for an Old Man." *Process Studies*, 44.1 (Spring/Summer 2015), 102–119.

———. "God and Pigment: John Updike on the Conservation of Meaning." *Religion and Literature* 36.3 (2004), 69–87.

———. "Visions of Reality and Meaning in the Thought of John Berger." *Ultimate Reality and Meaning*, 25.3 (2002), 168–184.

———. "Whitehead, Trauma, and the Presence of God." *Process Studies*, 42.1 (Spring/Summer 2013), 132–151.

Dixon, Graham. *Caravaggio: A Life Sacred and Profane*. New York: W.W. Norton, 2012.

Doepke, Frederick C. *The Kinds of Things: A Theory of Personal Identity Based on Transcendental Argument*. Chicago: Open Court, 1996.

Dunne, John S. *A Search for God in Time and Memory*. Notre Dame, IN: University of Notre Dame Press, 1977.

———. *The Way of All the Earth: Experiments in Truth and Religion*. Notre Dame, IN: University of Notre Dame Press, 1978.

Dyson, Freeman J. *Infinite in All Directions*. New York: Harper, 2004.

Elkins, James. *Pictures and Tears*. New York: Routledge, 2001.

Erikson, Erik. Robert Coles, ed. *The Erik Erikson Reader*. New York: W.W. Norton, 2001.

Fox, George. *The Journal of George Fox*. Richmond, IN: Friends Press, 2006.

Funk, Robert. *Jesus as Precursor*. Missoula: Scholars Press, 1997.

Gresham, John. *Nightmare Alley*. New York: New York Review of Books, 2006.

Harries, Karsten. *Infinity and Perspective*, Cambridge: MIT Press, 2001.

Hartshorne, Charles. *Anselm's Discovery: A Reexamination of the Ontological Proof of God's Existence*. New York: Open Court, 1991.

Jones, Serene. *Trauma and Grace*. Louisville: Westminster John Knox, 2009.

Kirk, Kenneth, *The Vision of God: The Christian Doctrine of the Summum Bonum*. New York: Morehouse Group, 1998.

Koch, Cristof. *Consciousness: Confessions of a Romantic Reductionist*. Cambridge: MIT Press, 2012.

Lewis. C. S. *Surprised By Joy*. New York: Harcourt, 1966.

———. *The Complete C. S. Lewis Signature Classics*. New York: HarperCollins, 2009.

Maugham, Somerset. *The Summing Up*. New York: Penguin, 1978.

McPhee, John. *Annals of the Former World*. New York: Farrar, Strauss and Giroux, 1998.

Merton, Thomas. *Conjectures of a Guilty Bystander*. New York: Image, 1966.

Mother Teresa. *Come Be My Light: The Private Writings of the "Saint of Calcutta."* New York: Doubleday, 2007.

Nelson, Shirley. *Fair, Clear, and Terrible*. Latham, New York: British American, 1989.

Niebuhr, H. Richard, *Radical Monotheism and Western Culture*. New York: Harper Row, 1970.

Nodelman, Sheldon. *The Rothko Chapel Paintings: Origin, Structure, Meaning*. Austin: University of Texas Press, 1997.

Novick, Leah. *On the Wings of Shekinah*. Wheaton, Ill: Theosophical, 2008.

O'Connor, Flannery. *Three*. New York: Signet, 1986.

Parfit, Derek. "Personal Identity," in John Perry, ed., *Personal Identity*. Berkeley, University of California Press, 1975.

Philips, J. B. *Your God is Too Small*. New York: Touchstone, 2004.

Phillips, D. Z. *The Problem of Evil and the Problem of God*. Minneapolis: Fortress, 2005.

Proust, Marcel. *Time Regained*. New York: Modern Library, 1999.

Rose, Gillian. *Love's Work: A Reckoning With Life*. New York: Schocken Books, 1995.

Rubenstein, Mary-Jane. *Strange Wonder: The Closure of Metaphysics and the Opening of Awe*. New York: Columbia, 2011.

———. *Worlds Without End: The Many Lives of the Universe*. New York: Columbia University Press, 2014.

Schama, Simon. *The Power of Art*. New York: HarperCollins, 2006.

Sells, Michael A. *Mystical Languages of Unsaying*. Chicago: U of Chicago Press, 1994.

Sibley, Brian. *Through the Shadowlands: The Love Story of C. S. Lewis and Joy Davidman*. Grand Rapids: Revell, 2005.

Soper, David Wesley, ed. *These Found the Way*. Louisville: Westminster, 1951.

Suchocki, Marge. *In God's Presence: Theological Reflections on Prayer*. New York: Chalice, 1996.

Taylor, Mark C. *Hiding*. Chicago: University of Chicago Press, 1997.

Tillich, Paul. *The Courage to Be*. New Haven: Yale University Press, 2014.

Tolan, Sandy. *The Lemon Tree: An Arab, a Jew, and the Heart of the Middle East*. New York: Bloomsbury, 2006.

Trisel, Brooke Alan. "Human Extinction and the Value of Our Efforts." *The Philosophical Forum: A Quarterly*, Vol. XXXV, No. 3, Fall, 2004.

Tyson, Neil DeGrasse. *Death by Black Holes*. New York: W.W. Norton, 2007.

Updike, John. *Just Looking*. New York: Knopf, 1989.

———. *Rabbit Angstrom: A Tetratology*. New York: Everyman Library, 1995.

———. *Seek My Face*. New York: Knopf, 2002.

———. *Self-Consciousness: Memoirs*. New York: Knopf, 1989.

Vendler, Helen. *Dickinson: Selected Poems and Commentaries*. Cambridge: Harvard University Press, 2010.

Whitehead, Alfred North. *Process and Reality*. 1929. Corrected ed. Eds. David Ray Griffin and Donald Sherburne. New York: Free Press, 1978.

Wiesel, Elie. *Night*. New York: Bantam, 1982.

Wiman, Christopher. *My Bright Abyss*. New York: Farrar, Straus and Giroux, 2014.

Made in the USA
Monee, IL
03 April 2020